# WHO KILLED CIVIL SOCIETY?

*The Rise of Big Government
and Decline of Bourgeois Norms*

Howard A. Husock

New York • London

First American edition published in 2019 by Encounter Books, an activity of Encounter for Culture and Education, Inc., a nonprofit, tax-exempt corporation. Encounter Books website address: www.encounterbooks.com

Manufactured in the United States and printed on acid-free paper. The paper used in this publication meets the minimum requirements of ANSI/NISO Z39.48–1992 (R 1997) (*Permanence of Paper*).

FIRST AMERICAN EDITION

LIBRARY OF CONGRESS CATALOGING-IN-PUBLICATION DATA
Names: Husock, Howard, author.
Title: Who killed civil society? : the rise of big government and decline of bourgeois norms / by Howard A. Husock.
Description: New York : Encounter Books, [2019] |
Includes bibliographical references and index.
Identifiers: LCCN 2019018888 (print) | LCCN 2019022308 (ebook) |
ISBN 9781641770583 (hardcover : alk. paper)
Subjects: LCSH: Social norms—United States. | Social service—United
States. | Civil society—United States. | United States—Social policy.
Classification: LCC HN90.M6 H87 2019  (print) | LCC HN90.M6  (ebook) |
DDC 303.3/7–dc23
LC record available at https://lccn.loc.gov/2019018888
LC ebook record available at https://lccn.loc.gov/2019022308

*Interior page design and composition: BooksByBruce.com*

*To my wife, Robin Henschel,*
*for her love and criticism;*
*my father, Bernard Husock,*
*for his example and assistance;*
*and my grandmother Ethel Levine,*
*for her encouragement.*

# CONTENTS

# How Civil Society
# Saved My Father

The biggest mystery of my childhood was the question of how my father had survived his. Though the details were fuzzy, the basic facts seemed clear: He was orphaned at age ten, in immigrant-heavy South Philadelphia, in the depth of the Great Depression. He had already been bounced from one home to another by his father, a widower overwhelmed by the responsibility of raising a son and a daughter before he himself died. Eventually, both my father, Bernard, and his older sister, Stella, entered foster care, a situation generally associated with a wide range of problems in adult life. And yet that would not be true of my father. At age eighteen he was going off by streetcar to engineering school. Then he joined the Navy to learn the new technology of radar. After the war, he went on to life in the suburban middle class and to the executive suite of a medium-sized business, with patents to show for his work.

What had made it possible? The intriguing explanation involved something he mentioned often but obliquely, something he called just "the Agency."

"Once a year," he would say, "the Agency took us to get a suit—one pair of long pants, one pair of knickers."

Or: "The Agency even paid to get my teeth fixed. That was before antibiotics, so you had to go once a week to get the root canal drained so it wouldn't get infected."

Or there was his oft-repeated story of his encounter, at age ten, with the Agency's psychologist, who after testing him remarked, "This one is a pretty smart kid." In the language of a later era, my father's self-esteem got a useful boost.

In a thousand ways, the world of my father's childhood amid the row houses of South Philly is a long-gone part of the American past—a world where fish were kept alive in the bathtub so they'd stay fresh, where teenagers enjoyed classical music, where sunflower seeds were the junk food of choice, where streetcars were the available transport, where boys and girls attended separate high schools. But the most distant aspect of that past is "the Agency." What was it, anyhow?

A search through archival records[1] confirmed that my father, from an early age, was raised without parents and without the support of public funds. Instead, a private organization called the Juvenile Aid Society, staffed in large part by volunteers, stepped in and provided a solid foundation for his life. This was the "Agency" that saved Bernard and Stella from homelessness. After interviewing multiple applicants as their potential foster families—at a time during the Depression when many were motivated by the prospect of extra income—the Agency chose so well that my father would remain close to the Grisbord family for the rest of his life, inviting his foster mother to his wedding and talking with Mrs. Grisbord's son, Manny, every Sunday into his eighties. Before the dawn of the taxpayer-funded "social service" state, the privately funded Agency gave my father the basis for his social mobility. Understanding what that consisted of is the inspiration for this book.

My father came of age at the end of an era when many of those in need were looked after and nurtured by organizations founded and managed by visionary individuals or communities. The voluntary associations of civil society helped not just children but entire families: immigrants and native-born, black and white, the poor and the disconnected, the jobless and the rural poor grappling with a new urban culture.

To be sure, local governments operated poorhouses in the nineteenth and early twentieth centuries, as well as orphanages and asylums. At times, government provided subsidies to private institutions (though not in the case of the Agency). But the needs of countless poor were met by private organizations, with some paid staff and many volunteers. During this time, a panoply of religiously inspired charitable organizations—Catholic, Protestant, Jewish—were helping children like my father, whether through orphanages or foster care or simple cash support for those in crisis. Similar organizations with no explicit religious affiliation also emerged from many different sources of inspiration. Philanthropically supported and staffed mostly by volunteers, they had no stake in the continuation of the problems they were addressing. With few paid staff members, they didn't need constant revenue streams to make payroll—a challenge that tempts modern charities to become government contractors and accept Washington's conditions for funding.

Other institutions also made a difference for my father. For instance, his public school, the South Philadelphia High School for Boys, imbued him with a love for classical music and Latin. But it was the Agency that was key.

The world of social service is dramatically different today, and in some ways better. As a result of the federal government's involvement since the Great Depression, and especially since the 1960s, those living in poverty are materially better off than their counterparts were a century ago. Food stamps, shelter, foster care, and health care (though not yet dental care) are funded by federal tax dollars. The story my father tells of a time when he and his sister scrounged for food and a place to sleep should, in theory, not be told today. Much of what the Agency offered to them is now provided by government, regardless of ethnicity or religious affiliation. This universal reach would not have been achievable by civil society organizations such as the Juvenile Aid Society.

But despite the massive scale and blanket coverage of the modern social service state, it fails to provide something essential that only civil society—operating independently from government revenue and its restraints—can offer: the modeling of habits and values that lay the foundation for upward social mobility and life as a contributor to one's community. In other words, only civil society can impart *norms*. It is norms, not material provisions, that lead to improved outcomes for the individual and society.

## Norms Matter

My father did not just survive his childhood; he went on to thrive as a productive, responsible adult. Those looking after him in his youth were concerned with much more than his physical well-being. As part and parcel of the Agency's approach, they sought to shape his values—to inculcate the norms that are sometimes mocked as "bourgeois"—in the belief that the right behaviors were as important as food and shelter in the long run. Volunteers visiting families were making sure that every child had his own bed and a place to study, but they were also emphasizing a list of personal virtues—published and distributed by the Agency—through which the children were to be uplifted.

- Self-respect
- Living according to fine and high principles
- The meaning of honor and confidence and trust
- Self-control and self-government
- The meaning of truth and honesty, and other cardinal virtues
- Good manners everywhere
- The reality of the moral law which cannot be violated without severe penalties[2]

The volunteers dispatched with that list were messengers from the middle and upper classes, tasked with teaching the right behaviors and habits to set the table for healthy living and future success.

As my father recalled, those general values translated into very specific guidance from Matilda Kohn Sternberger, the wealthy widow who traveled by a chauffeur-driven Cadillac from fashionable Rittenhouse Square to his foster home for regular visits. There is no doubt that Mrs. Sternberger herself subscribed to the values she was called upon to transmit, and she had high expectations for their benefits. A transcript of a Juvenile Aid Society board meeting on January 17, 1933, includes this comment from her: "I think that children are willing and anxious to become independent and if we can get them young enough they can get a very normal attitude toward life and their responsibilities."[3] Mrs. Sternberger appeared to assume that my father would be better off in adulthood as a result of her influence, and she emphasized that he should plan to make his own contributions to charity when the time came. In fact, I recall his making phone calls every year for the United Jewish Appeal in his adopted city of Cleveland.

The virtues that the Juvenile Aid Society was promoting had not been tested by social science; they can be understood as a version of the values promoted by Aristotle, including courage, temperance, honor, and truthfulness. Still, modern data analysis suggests that the adoption of bourgeois values leads to a better life. One good example comes from the work published in 2013 by Ron Haskins and Isabelle Sawhill, social scientists at the Brookings Institution in Washington, D.C. By studying decades of data, they discovered the "cure" for poverty that Mrs. Sternberger would have known intuitively: finish high school, get a job, and get married before you have babies. Their term for these norms in combination is *the success sequence*. From their survey of the research, they concluded that those who follow all three "rules" in succession have a 70 percent chance of earning a middle-class income, and just a 5 percent chance of living in poverty.[4]

The research of Haskins and Sawhill built upon groundbreaking work published in 1994 by the sociologists Sara McLanahan and Gary Sandefur, which focused on one aspect of the "success sequence": the importance of marriage for the prospects of children. McLanahan and Sandefur used "nationally representative data sets" to compare life outcomes for children who grew up in a home with two biological parents, with a single parent, and with a parent and a stepparent. A summary of their findings reported:

> McLanahan and Sandefur found that children who did not live with both biological parents were roughly twice as likely to be poor, to have a birth outside of marriage, to have behavioral and psychological problems, and to not graduate from high school. Other studies have reported associations between family structure and child health outcomes. For example, one study found children living in single-parent homes were more likely to experience health problems, such as accidents, injuries, and poisonings.[5]

Subsequent research by other social scientists adds support to these findings. For example, Wendy Wang and W. Bradford Wilcox examined the "success sequence" in 2017, and concluded:

Even millennials from low-income families are more likely to flourish if they married before having children: 71 percent who married before having children made it into the middle or higher end of the income distribution by the time they are age 28–34. By comparison, only 41 percent of millennials from lower-income families who had children first made it into the middle or higher end of the distribution when they reached ages 28–34.[6]

The point here is not only the demonstrated importance of married, two-parent families, both for spouses and for their children. This is just one aspect of a broader point: adopting the right behavioral norms makes for a better life. *Norms matter*.

In my father's time, it was acknowledged that bourgeois norms were an essential key to upward mobility, or at least to a healthy, stable life, not just for children in foster care but for the poor in general, for immigrants, and for all those grappling with the uncertainties of an industrial economy. That's why private organizations like the Juvenile Aid Society were founded at the local level and supported by committed communities. The goals of those civil society organizations went well beyond the determination of need and the delivery of material assistance, to focus on introducing and inculcating moral norms as the basis for a productive, successful, satisfying adult life.

The implicit message was that if they adopted the right values and habits, those who were "at risk," in contemporary parlance, could thrive chiefly (though not exclusively) through their own effort. This principle has faded away. Pop psychology may have embraced "self-empowerment" as the key to success, but those who struggle are often told that institutional barriers are to blame. By contrast, no one would have told my father that an entrenched elite looked askance at Jewish immigrants and stood in the way of his advancement (although in some ways that was true).

Today there are legions of children in a situation not unlike that of my father and his sister. In fact, the population of children entering foster care has increased by somewhere between 15 and 30 percent since 2010, likely due in part to opioid-related parental neglect, and outcomes for children in the foster system remain bleak despite more than a half century of government involvement. One study showed that children who spent time in foster care between 1988 and 1998 experienced rates of post-traumatic stress disorder similar to those of combat veterans; they used the General Equivalency Exam to complete high school at more than six times the rate of the general population; and had below-average rates of employment and insurance coverage. Our child welfare system, as Richard Gelles has written, is "a frustrating, dysfunctional system that cannot ensure that the children who most need protection will be safe."[7]

Is anyone bringing these children the uplifting message that Mrs. Sternberger brought to my father? Does anyone still put a premium on the kind of norms she strove to impart?

## WHERE HAVE ALL THE CIVIL SOCIETY INSTITUTIONS GONE?

Today we are still concerned about social norms, though the terms have changed. Once we spoke of "temperance" and the problem of alcohol; now we discuss "substance abuse" and especially opioids. Once we deplored "pauperism" and "tramps"; now we worry about declining participation in the workforce and chronic homelessness. Once we spoke of illegitimacy and immoral sexual behavior; today we express concern about single parenthood and the "at-risk" children in such households. Once we worried about vice and immorality; today we decry hate and bullying.

Something else has changed besides the terminology: we no longer have institutional equivalents of the Agency to foster social norms. With the rise of what I am calling the social service state and its eclipse of civil society institutions like my father's savior, the norms that provide the foundation for upward mobility have lacked a bully pulpit—and societal trends over the same period of time have not been encouraging.

The number of children raised without two biological parents in the home, like my father and his sister after their parents' deaths, has ballooned since their day, and even people who are agnostic about social mores must acknowledge that such children suffer higher rates of poverty, substance abuse, and poor physical and emotional health than children raised by both their parents. The Census Bureau's *Statistical Abstract of the United States* reported that the marriage rate was 40 percent lower in 2008 than it was 1940, and the divorce rate 175 percent higher. The rate of out-of-wedlock birth increased by a factor of ten between 1960 and 2008. The National Institute on Drug Abuse reported that by 2018, drug overdose deaths had soared to a staggering 70,000 a year, having doubled over the preceding decade.[8] Men between the ages of 25 and 54 are increasingly not attached to the labor force at all. Through the 1950s and 1960s, notes the Harvard economist Edward Glaeser, 95 percent of these "prime-age" men were regularly employed, but the proportion of those not employed has risen steadily since 1970, to the point that over 15 percent of "prime-age" men were out of the labor force in 2017. "Nowadays," Glaeser remarks, "most non-employed men have given up looking for work."[9]

Any number of explanations for these trends merit credence: Low-skilled employment opportunities in manufacturing have dwindled. Wages are failing to keep up with inflation. And as Charles Murray observed in his 1984 classic, *Losing Ground*, the role of low-income men has been diminished since the mothers of their children qualified more easily for public assistance.

But the worrying social trends cannot be ascribed wholly to economic factors. The United States, in fact, has made dramatic progress in living standards since the New Deal era. In 1940, nearly half of residential structures lacked indoor plumbing; by 1990, that was true of only 1 percent. Poverty in America today is relative, not abject.

To be sure, social scientists disagree as to whether there has been a decline in "upward mobility," defined as earning more than one's parents.[10] But my concern is not confined to economic considerations such as whether one has adequate income for food and shelter, or whether one's income is some percentage points higher than one's parents. I am convinced—by experience and by data—that those who are exposed to the right norms (and internalize them) are more likely to be able to improve their own socioeconomic status. But whether they do or not, living a structured life of work, marriage, family, and community engagement is, in my view, a valuable end in itself.

## FORMATIVE, NOT REFORMATIVE

Civil society seems to have lost the will to promote the norms that guided my father and so many others—to do the ordinary marketing, if you will, of bourgeois norms. In the era of my father's youth and in much of the nineteenth century, the middle and upper classes reinforced their own belief in such values by encouraging the poor and disadvantaged to adopt them, offering the keys to the kingdom of achievement and satisfaction. Volunteers "settled" in poor and immigrant neighborhoods to model good habits and teach English and the importance of citizenship.

Today we might wring our hands over the decline of marriage and the upsurge in out-of-wedlock birth, but we dare not "preach" or "judge" others. Charles Murray has written of the need to start preaching again: "Married, educated people who work hard and conscientiously raise their kids shouldn't hesitate to voice their disapproval of those who defy these norms. When it comes to marriage and the work ethic, the new upper class must start preaching what it practices."[11]

Another of America's most trenchant social observers notes that today's social landscape, increasingly segregated in economic terms, offers little chance for healthy norms to spread to those who might benefit from a constructive example. As Robert Putnam has written, "rich Americans and poor Americans are living, learning, and raising children in increasingly separate and unequal worlds, removing the stepping-stones to upward mobility—college-going classmates or cousins or middle-class neighbors, who might take a working-class kid from the neighborhood under their wing."[12]

During my father's childhood, better-off Americans mixed their lives with those of the poor through the institutions of civil society. For instance, a nineteenth-century crusader from a privileged background named Charles Loring Brace opened a lodging house on New York's Lower East Side for newsboys and bootblacks who roamed the streets, sometimes in gangs. In the Newsboys' Lodging House they were exhorted to "work early and late," to "be quick," to deal honestly with everyone, for the true way to wealth was by "constant saving and hard work." At the least, they would "have no reason to be ashamed or fear the law" if they followed this counsel.[13]

In Illinois, a daughter of small-town affluence named Jane Addams moved to Chicago's immigrant-filled West Side to found Hull House, where idealistic and well-to-do young people would "settle" among those who might profit from their example. Addams believed that the way to help immigrants adjust to a new life was to "bring them in contact with a better type of Americans," while encouraging them to preserve what was valuable from their native culture.[14]

Settlement houses such as Hull House were intended to uplift whole neighborhoods, while "friendly visitors" such as Mrs. Sternberger brought to individual households a similar message of uplift through discipline, temperance, and education. The social work pioneer Mary Richmond, herself raised by her poor and widowed grandmother in Baltimore, saw that "friendly visiting" could disseminate such constructive values as honesty, industry, and sobriety. She aimed to "release energy and initiative" among the poor, and to cultivate "higher and better wants and saner social relations."[15]

Today these women might be branded as elitists or condescending "Lady Bountifuls." But they were confident in their belief that the values that guided their own families could help the poor to improve their lives—or to "reach their full potential," as it might be put today. And they did not hesitate to say so.

There is little doubt that the expression of such convictions has fallen out of fashion. For example, in 2018 the *Wall Street Journal* described the effort of one New York City educator to deter out-of-wedlock childbearing among high school students, since births to poor unmarried mothers presented "a huge obstacle to improving achievement." But as the *Journal* noted, "Many school leaders hesitate to make this claim, for fear of moralizing."[16]

We should not shrink from just such moralizing because—to use contemporary language again—it can actually empower people. "Middle-class morality" and "bourgeois values" should be seen as "sensible and commonsensical advice that really does benefit the poor," as Joel Schwartz has written, in appreciation of the work done by Brace and Addams, among others.[17] Dispensing this advice is not the proper role of government, however. Agencies of government dispense tax dollars as democratically directed, in response to social problems, but their purpose is not to promote values or set personal norms. The Department of Health and Human Services' Administration for Children and Families alone distributes some $53 billion annually to a panoply of social service providers—to protect children whose parents are drug abusers, to help runaways and the homeless, to discourage adolescent pregnancy. There is a common thread to all such programs: they focus on what I call the "reformative" rather than the "formative." They are designed to remedy problems, not to prevent them from appearing in the first place.

## THE PROBLEM OF GOVERNMENT AND THE FORMATIVE

Government at all levels has now become the funder of social services, outsourcing to local nonprofits the job of distributing tax dollars, which influence the activities of those organizations. The Urban Institute has reported that, as of 2012,

- government agencies entered into approximately 350,000 contracts and grants with about 56,000 nonprofit organizations;
- on average, nonprofits have six contracts and/or grants per organization; the median is three; and
- governments paid $137 billion to nonprofit organizations for services.[18]

These figures represent the capture of civil society by government-funded social services, focused on treatment, therapy, and the political aims of "social justice."

When government extends its reach into what was once the domain of civil society, the moral influence of the latter inevitably withers, as the sociologist Nathan Glazer observed in *The Limits of Social Policy*. He pointed out "the simple reality that every piece of social policy substitutes for some traditional arrangement, whether good or bad, a new arrangement in which public authorities take over, at least in part, the role of the family, of the ethnic and neighborhood group, of voluntary associations."[19] Moreover, with government capture comes a shift of emphasis, so that energy and resources that could be spent on formative efforts are instead channeled into reformative programs.

While reformative operations such as the Administration for Children and Families (ACF) distribute tens of billions of dollars, relatively little goes into programs aimed at preventing problems from emerging. For example, the YMCA, with an enduring focus on exercise and good health (although no longer on faith-inspired norms, as in the nineteenth century), spends $155 million annually through its local chapters across the

United States. The Boys and Girls Clubs of America, with a similar focus, spend $1.73 billion. The Boy Scouts and Girl Scouts of America spend less than $500 million. These organizations, which are formative in their approach, operate on a tiny fraction of the ACF budget.

At the same time, the profession of social work no longer promotes the idea that the right attitudes and habits can help the poor and working-class to succeed. Today's social workers believe that only structural changes in the economy will prevent the problems associated with poverty. The emphasis has shifted away from direct interaction with those in need, toward what Mary Richmond disapprovingly called "wholesale" rather than "retail" reform.[20]

In twenty-first-century America, most of Matilda Sternberger's successors are employed by the government or by organizations that operate under government contract. They don't seek to impart the same sort of values that Mrs. Sternberger—a volunteer who identified herself as a social worker—taught my father. If they are teaching a set of values, it is a political and economic worldview in which the problems of the individual stem from systemic oppression. This worldview is laid bare in a 2012 textbook description of the profession for graduate students in social work:

> Social workers recognize the extent to which a culture's structures and values may oppress, marginalize, alienate, or create or enhance privilege and power.... Social workers understand the forms and mechanisms of oppression and discrimination...and engage in practices that advance social and economic justice.[21]

This is a dispiriting message, implying that the odds are stacked against those of modest means and from minority backgrounds—that the chances of success are beyond one's own control. It's a long way from the message of the Juvenile Aid Society. In the professional social service world of today's America, "norms" are rarely if ever referenced; indeed, they are not mentioned in any of the ten major training areas outlined by the Council on Social Work Education.[22]

I am not arguing that government should be promoting bourgeois norms through its financial support for social services. When government speaks about morals, it risks creating division and destabilization. Consider the response to an effort by the administration of New

York City to mount a public information campaign to discourage teen pregnancy. Robert Doar, appointed by Mayor Michael Bloomberg in 2007 as the Human Resources Administration's commissioner, was particularly concerned about high levels of birth to unmarried mothers, which has been shown to increase the likelihood of a lifetime spent in poverty, not only for the mother herself but also for her children. Doar proposed a campaign against teen pregnancy to Mayor Bloomberg, who was known for his public health campaigns to reduce smoking and obesity. The official city press release pointedly declared: "It is well past time when anyone can afford to be value-neutral when it comes to teen pregnancy." A series of powerful and emotional subway advertisements followed, emphasizing the poor life-chances of babies born out of wedlock.

But what Doar understood to be incontrovertible antipoverty idealism drew a chorus of disapproval. Planned Parenthood's New York vice president was "shocked and taken aback" by the tone of the campaign, claiming, "It's not teen pregnancies that cause poverty, but poverty that causes teen pregnancy." National Public Radio reported that Mayor Bloomberg was "mired in another health controversy," as the new campaign had "provoked negative reactions from every quarter—the right, the left, mayoral candidates and even health advocates." The *New York Times* headlined its analysis of the program this way: "In fighting teenage pregnancy, the folly of shame and blame." The initiative was, according to the *Times*, "a jarringly judgmental advertising campaign that aims to shame teenage parents and scare teenage girls who are not yet parents by warning that really bad consequences await should they get pregnant." Michael Powell further noted in his *New York Times* column that teen pregnancy rates in New York had steadily fallen prior to the campaign, and he suggested that the city government not only was sending the wrong message but was the wrong messenger. "When from time to time I find myself in black and Latino churches," Powell wrote, "I often hear a social message that is usefully middle-class, and aimed at encouraging men and women to recognize their responsibilities to one another." He criticized Bloomberg's inner circle for harboring the conceit "that this city administration alone speaks truth."[23]

Not everyone disapproved of Doar's efforts, of course. While it has become controversial to be "judgmental about anything," as Ron Haskins observes, the message of the campaign was in line with his own research at Brookings, and particularly with the "success sequence," in which childbearing is postponed until after marriage. Indeed, Robert Doar was not wrong in the view that he sought to promote, but rather in using government as the vehicle for doing so. Traditionally it is civil society that has fostered constructive norms. Imagine federal agencies launching campaigns for social norms: Which set of norms would be represented? To the extent that the "success sequence" is promoted, notes Haskins, it is by civil society groups.[24]

Civil society should once again be the agency for shaping norms and influencing behavior. This work should be done "retail, not wholesale," as the political scientist James Q. Wilson wrote in 2003 concerning how to encourage marriage as a central aspect of bourgeois values. It must be done "by families and churches and neighborhoods and the media, not by tax breaks or government subsidies."[25]

## ONLY NORMS LEAD TO SCALE

Americans still care about the norms that influence the individual's behavior and the consequences for society. But our language for talking about norms has changed, and so have the means for disseminating them.

My primary aim is to tell the story of that change, first recounting the development of an American civil society dedicated to the propagation of constructive social norms, and then tracing its gradual transformation and decline. The story includes the lives and times of several important visionaries: Charles Loring Brace, founder of New York's Children's Aid Society; Jane Addams, leader of the influential settlement house movement and founder of Chicago's Hull House; Mary Richmond, who promoted the professionalization of social work while striving to prevent it from losing the Victorian-era values she cherished.

Then came the reformers who undid the work of promoting formative values. Grace Abbott, a Progressive-era daughter of small-town Iowa, led a new type of government agency, the federal Children's Bureau, which was created to study social problems and then became an advocate of government funding to solve them. Wilbur Cohen, a grocer's son from Milwaukee, successfully directed millions, then billions of dollars to a social service state built on a Progressive vision that undermined civil society by trying to improve upon it.

I am motivated to tell their stories because I believe that the formative norms of the past are necessary for our future. One contemporary who shares this view is Geoffrey Canada, who acutely feels the absence of constructive norms and recognizes the consequences for individuals and society. He embodies my optimism for a reinvigorated civil society that teaches norms, having built a new and influential social service model called the Harlem Children's Zone. Funded primarily by private philanthropy, it is devoted to inculcating what Canada explicitly calls "middle-class values" in disadvantaged, minority-group poor children.

In his book *Reaching Up for Manhood*, Canada writes, "We should view work, hard work, as a necessary rite of passage for boys early in their lives. We must teach them that there is nothing demeaning in working hard, whether it's for money or not."[26] This statement could easily have found a place in *The Dangerous Classes of New York and Twenty Years' Work Among Them*, published by Charles Loring Brace in 1880. And there is solid reason to believe that Canada's thinking has had a positive impact. At a time when only 40 percent of all black high school graduates are on track to receive any sort of college degree within six years, the figure is 78 percent for Harlem Children's Zone students.

Others too have hit upon the insight that the early inculcation of healthy norms is key to a satisfying life for individuals and to a productive society. I have met such people through my own work over the past twenty years at New York City's Manhattan Institute, where I lead a project to identify nonprofit, nongovernmental, civil society organizations that are effective in assisting the disadvantaged. In Atlanta, the Fugees Academy, led by Luma Mufleh, specializes in educating the children of refugees, "helping students and their families manage some of the challenges of life in a new country," as the school puts it. Mufleh is herself a refugee from Jordan. This work represents the settlement house tradition, still alive in American life. In southern Ohio, Alice Ely Chapman's education foundation uses after-school guidance and tutoring to build a "work ethic" in a region devastated by parental drug use and disability. Academic progress has followed, as Ely Chapman students have gone on to graduate from high school at a disproportionately high rate.[27] In Dallas, Reid Porter turned his back on a remunerative corporate law career to start Advocates for Community Transformation, which has used the law to shut down dozens of "drug houses" that are hubs of crime and violence in the city's poor neighborhoods. In Shreveport, Louisiana, the Community Renewal organization recruits married black couples such as Emmitt and Sharpel Welch to run a "friendship house," modeling middle-class mores and providing guidance in a historically poor African American neighborhood.

These are not groups that aim to meet short-term targets, such as year-over-year declines in crime statistics or illegitimacy rates. Rather, they promote norms of timeless value—marriage, the work ethic, friendship, independence combined with community-mindedness—whose benefits truly emerge over the long term. Such organizations are started by people who want to provide the disadvantaged with the tools for their own uplift, and who are confident that those who have internalized the norms they promote will in time lead better lives as a result.

Many data-focused donors to these and other civil society organizations worry that their programs touch too few lives to have much effect. They ask how the organizations plan to bring their good ideas "to scale." This line of questioning tempts civil society's institutions to pursue handsomely funded government contracts and accept the condition that they address existing problems, patching holes in our ever-fraying social fabric. But in a society whose norms have been rent, no amount of funding is enough to repair all the damage.

In fact, the only way to achieve scale is through norms. While helping those who leave prison is undoubtedly good, it is more effective to discourage even the small offenses that lead to contact with the criminal justice system. Providing single parents with extra resources can help them, but it is far more beneficial to discourage those who are not married from having children in the first place. Programs to correct manifest social problems are always likely to be overwhelmed by need. In contrast, the promotion of healthy norms can achieve scale by influencing not only those directly touched, but many others who see the broadcast example of "bourgeois" behavior and the evidence of its value.

Only norms lead to scale, and only civil society can transmit norms. Were a restored civil society to focus on the formative rather than the reformative—on building social and behavioral norms—it would make government-funded social programs less necessary.

The title of this book may be hyperbolic in suggesting that American civil society is dead. In many ways, it continues to thrive, especially at the local level: in parent-teacher groups, historical societies, mentoring groups, local sports leagues, and the like. This book charts the withering of a particular *kind* of civil society organization, one that is dedicated to promoting the social norms that enable the poor to rise and prosper, and that help bind the American social fabric. While the growth of government efforts to address behavioral problems and their aftermath—at great expense—cannot help but do some good, a problem-centered focus is simply no substitute for the willingness of civil society to promote healthy norms. That is the part of civil society we have worked to kill, and Americans suffer as a result.

A new wave of civil society leaders and organizations is needed in response to persistent social ills and emergent new problems. Such leaders and organizations need to be recognized and supported by their communities. I hope this book will not only reveal the untold story of past pioneers in fostering norms and spotlight the work of their modern-day heirs, but also inspire more efforts of this kind in the future.

# I

# CHARLES LORING BRACE: "TO AVERT RATHER THAN CURE"

T he issue of how to help the poor has always been a fundamentally challenging one for the United States. In modern times, it is treated as a matter of public policy, to be decided through debate and implemented by government. But through much of American history, private initiatives and organizations mattered as much or more than public policy.

The place of behavioral norms in dealing with poverty is a particularly fraught question. Maintaining that one's own behavior can change one's situation for the better is a highly contentious proposition, given that many people find themselves in dire circumstances through no fault of their own. But American history is shaped by stories of people who have believed they could improve their own condition, however challenging the circumstances.

At the same time, the idea of a societal responsibility to mitigate poverty has long been a part of the American tradition. *From the Depths* (1956), by the social welfare historian Robert Bremner, describes an American view of poverty as something "unnatural" in such a fortunate land:

> In contrast to the peoples of less fortunate lands, who have accepted poverty as inevitable, Americans have tended to regard it as an abnormal condition. Our belief that want is unnatural and

unnecessary originated in a hopeful view of human nature. It has been strengthened by our faith in the unlimited resources of the New World and... by pride in the productive achievements of the American economic system.[1]

From this perspective, poverty is "shameful" not for the poor, but for a wealthy society that allows it to persist.

Because of this view, there has always been some level of direct government assistance to people in need. Indeed, long before the United States became a wealthy nation, providing food and shelter for the needy was part of civic life, starting with the Puritans. A Massachusetts law of 1744 required all towns to establish poorhouses. By the early nineteenth century, such institutions were maintained by localities across the country. In New York, an "almshouse" was located on Blackwell's (later Roosevelt) Island. In Boston, there was one at the corner of Park and Beacon, alongside the Boston Common. In Philadelphia, the almshouse was in the block bounded by Third, Fourth, Spruce, and Pine streets. Before there was a safety net of federally funded assistance programs, the needy were not altogether ignored, but public relief had a limited aim: "to prevent starvation and death from exposure as economically as possible."[2] The idea that the right interventions could somehow improve the prospects of the poor had not yet taken hold.

The "poor law" tradition would gradually lead to a full-blown "safety net," offering a wide range of financial assistance for people with low incomes, from food stamps (the Supplemental Nutritional Assistance Program) to old-age pensions through the Social Security Act. Debate has always surrounded the federal safety net's development and maintenance: Is it too stingy or too generous? Should it be cash or select goods and services? Should those who receive federally funded health insurance (Medicaid) be required to work? Should "nutritional assistance" be confined to the purchase of what are deemed "healthy" foods?

The question of this safety net's appropriate form has long dogged political discourse, but a basic consensus has emerged that much economic hardship in a modern economy is "situational," the result of innovation and disruption, as well as the vagaries of the business cycle. One can be ready and able to work, and still be caught in the downdraft, whether because of global financial events or technological advances—perhaps including artificial intelligence and robots, as some futurists suppose.

Alongside the "poor law" tradition that led to "safety net" programs, there was a parallel American tradition whose atrophy is a central theme of this book. When the United States was still far from capable of implementing large-scale income redistribution, another strand of action began to develop: one predicated on the idea that upward mobility could be encouraged by influencing the attitudes and actions of people who are not well off.

In early nineteenth-century Boston, a Unitarian minister, Joseph Tuckerman, began acting as pastor to people who were "living as a caste, cut off from those in more favored circumstances."[3] Tuckerman raised funds from the better-off for a "Poor's Purse" to provide financial assistance, but he also sought to mitigate the problems of illiteracy and delinquency. In New York, in 1843, the British-born merchant Robert Hartley founded the Association for Improving the Condition of the Poor, which built a far-reaching system of "friendly visiting" to those in need. The visitors might give emergency assistance, such as coal or food, and would offer counsel in the vocabulary of norms: "piety, total abstinence, frugality, and industry."[4] Their mission included distributing copies of "The Way to Wealth," Benjamin Franklin's advice from 1758:

> Sloth makes all things difficult, but industry all easy; and He that riseth late must trot all day, and shall scarce overtake his business at night; while Laziness travels so slowly, that Poverty soon overtakes him. Drive thy business, let not that drive thee; and Early to bed, and early to rise, makes a man healthy, wealthy, and wise....
>
> So what signifies wishing and hoping for better times? We may make these times better, if we bestir ourselves. Industry need not wish, and he that lives upon hopes will die fasting.... If we are industrious, we shall never starve; for, At the working man's house hunger looks in, but dares not enter.

This counsel reflects the idea that one's character and life choices powerfully affect one's prospects. It is a deeply American view, influenced by Protestant theology, and predicated on opportunity and abundance. But giving a practical form to this belief required action on the part of individuals willing to dedicate themselves to uplifting the needy. These people would be missionaries of a sort, carrying a message by which the poor could be "trained to self-reliance and habits of industry," as the Philadelphia Children's Aid Society put it in 1882 with respect to homeless and neglected children.

Applied to adults, such a mission might sound condescending to modern ears. But throughout American history there have always been waves of immigrants who are new to the demands of a modern urban economy. My father's parents came from a tiny agrarian village in Ukraine and likely faced assimilation challenges similar to those experienced by southern and eastern European immigrants who had left behind a rural subsistence life. There have also been native-born groups who find difficulty in adjusting to new conditions. For instance, former sharecroppers moving to northern cities from the South faced a daunting transition. Their modern-day successors, including immigrants from Mexico and from Central and South America, are drawn to the magnet of American prosperity, and many arrive with limited education and little understanding of American mores.

Intervention in the lives of those who struggle, beyond emergency assistance, need not be seen as a judgment on their native culture or their personal behavior. Rather, it should be regarded as social preparation: helping those in a new situation understand bourgeois norms, rules, and social cues, and recognize their value as a springboard to upward mobility. Norms such as discipline and sobriety are important for all strata of society, of course—and one cannot assume that affluent households have consistently prepared their children to succeed through healthy norms. But the poor, and especially the children of the poor, face the most serious consequences if they fail to adapt to circumstances, and often they are not yet familiar with the norms of a modern, industrial society.

Recognizing this reality prompted Charles Loring Brace to start an organization based on the idea that the children of the poor could rise both socially and economically with the right preparation. He was the first major figure to build such an organization with national reach. In the early nineteenth century, devoting one's professional life to assisting the poor in this way was unprecedented. Brace helped invent the idea of such a career when he founded the Children's Aid Society.

Brace's family background might not have suggested the particular path he took, though it was an upbringing that would have encouraged

original thinking. He was born in 1836 into the education-valuing culture of New England. His Puritan family roots went back to Hartford,
Connecticut, in the 1660s. A great-grandfather, Abel Brace, was an officer
in the Revolutionary War. Other family members served as legislators,
clergymen, and journalists; his father, John Brace, edited the *Hartford
Courant*. The Brace family was not wealthy, but Charles's childhood,
first in Litchfield and then in Hartford, was nonetheless bucolic. As a
boy living in close proximity to lakes and streams, he developed a lifelong passion for trout fishing. He was home-schooled by his father, who
tutored him two hours each day, often on the plays of Shakespeare and
the adventure novels of Walter Scott. As his daughter would write, "The
Greek and Roman histories with which the course began were acted out
in the boy's imagination by the aid of acorns, with which he represented
contending armies."[5]

Education had been the family's business. In Brace's earliest years,
his father was headmaster of the Litchfield Female Academy, founded
by two of Brace's aunts and dedicated to what was then certainly a novel
goal: the education of girls beyond the elementary grades. Brace himself
became fluent in German, Spanish, French, and Latin. A lifelong friend
of his since boyhood was Frederick Law Olmsted, who would go on
to fame as the nation's premier landscape architect and the designer of
New York's Central Park (and whose regular letters to Brace addressed
him as "Charley"). As Brace gained international renown for his work
with New York's poor, he would become a friend to John Stuart Mill
and Charles Darwin.

His ideas, germinated in a childhood of modest comfort and New
England Christianity, translated into direct assistance on a significant
scale and represented a new approach to addressing the problems of the
poor. Its animating precept: that the poor, especially the immigrant poor,
needed preparation to cope with the demands of ever-changing markets
and the stresses of striving for upward mobility. Brace also believed that
bad habits were not a reflection of immorality, but the result of a failure
by the better-off to provide guidance and help.

These beliefs led Brace, in 1853, to launch the Children's Aid Society
in New York and undertake a long list of signature projects through the
privately supported organization. He began by setting up the Newsboys'
Lodging House to assist the newsboys, bootblacks, and other children of
New York's streets. Eventually there were six lodging houses and a range

of other initiatives throughout New York, in which Brace would succor 170,000 children over a period of twenty-five years.[6] Like his father, Brace did not neglect girls, but established a network of "industrial schools" to help them avoid the all too well-known risks of street life. This was at a time when education was not compulsory, and Brace estimated that the number of illiterates above the age of ten in New York had reached "the astounding height of 241,152." The Children's Aid Society also sent thousands of New York children west on "orphan trains" to be adopted by farm families, who were expected to impart the sorts of values that the organization stood for.

Brace conceived and embraced a mission to help those born into poverty adopt the personal values he believed would enable them to escape it. He regarded education, not charity, as the best way to cure "pauperism." Like others who followed in his path, he did not assume that a combination of good character and education was a guarantee against privation, but believed that it provided the means to take advantage of economic opportunity.

Addressing the Harvard Divinity School in 1881, Brace summarized his approach in nearly three decades of working with what he unabashedly called New York's "dangerous classes." He was speaking at the invitation of Harvard's president, Charles Eliot (himself on the cusp of transforming the institution from a regional finishing school to a national leader in higher education). Brace observed that America's cities—and particularly New York, "that great entrepot of immigration"—were filled with "young ruffians... the products of accident, ignorance and vice." And this "great multitude of ignorant, untrained, passionate, irreligious boys and young men" had become "the dangerous class of our city." He cited root causes of disorder that would resonate with diagnoses of social ills in our own day, including "the neglect of the marriage tie and the subsequent breakup of family life."[7]

Brace went on to describe the method embodied in his Children's Aid Society: "First then, we at the outset [seek] to help by encouraging self-help; that is, we seek to influence character, as well as to supply wants." His aims were both practical and transcendent: to inspire "respect of the good and the love of moral beauty," and by this means "to avert rather than cure the diseases of society."[8] The phrase "avert rather than cure" is key to understanding how Brace touched the lives of tens of thousands of adolescents.

An insight into the roots of Brace's mission to the poor can be found in an extensive volume of his letters preserved by his daughter Emma. While he was studying at Yale in 1843, he wrote to his father of his decision to take up "moral philosophy" because of its emphasis on "the principles of the duties and obligations of man." But his focus would be practical, and he reported that his classmates already referred to him as "the philanthropist." After earning his undergraduate degree, he taught in private schools to finance his study for the ministry at Yale. (In keeping with the Connecticut Dissenter tradition, he was a Methodist, not a "high church" Episcopalian.) He traveled on a shoestring through Europe to see firsthand the conditions of its poor and to meet its clergy. He wrote of living on fifty cents a day in Berlin while still cultivating a circle of friends that included the scientist Alexander von Humboldt.

Brace was on fire with political passions. His letters expressed outrage over the Fugitive Slave Law, which was intended to force people living in free states to return escaped slaves to captivity. In a letter to Olmsted ("Fred") in 1848, he declared, "If I could do something to lessen on American soil that curse of slavery, I shall be satisfied. I feel the inconsistency, the injustice of it, the longer I live."[9] In another letter he wrote, "I would rather see a dozen Unions broken than be personally responsible for the slavery of another human being."[10]

He was alive to theoretical economics and outspoken in favor of free trade, although his fellow New Englanders had long favored tariffs in their global competition with British industry. "Mutual commerce uniting nations [is worth] more than a hundred treaties!" he wrote. "Human selfishness at length doing what benevolence has never done, 'making wars to cease on the face of the earth.'"[11]

Brace first came to New York (where he visited Olmsted at his Staten Island home) in order to minister to inmates at the city's prison on Blackwell's Island, but "a few months' experience convinced him that the effort to reform adults was well-nigh hopeless," his daughter recounted.[12] He came to a conclusion that would shape his life's work: "It soon became clear," wrote Brace himself, "that whatever was done must be done in the source and origin of the evil—prevention not cure."[13]

He therefore decided he must immerse himself in the lives of New York's poor. Such a decision would become more commonplace—indeed, even a career choice—over the course of American history, but it was quite a novelty at the time. A representative of America's oldest stock, a direct descendant of colonial New Englanders, took it upon himself to minister to its newest immigrants by enunciating and promoting the norms of the society they were joining. "I want to raise up the outcast and the homeless, to go down among those who have no friend or helper."[14]

As he contemplated founding the Children's Aid Society to "raise up the outcast," this was his view of New York:

> The childish crime and poverty of New York had reached an incredible extent in 1853, when these labors began. Vagrant children swarmed the streets; crime among them was a profession; every species of street-trade was employed by them for a support; many hundreds slept in boxes, barns, cellars and under stair-ways, and so common was vagrancy and its necessary result—criminal life—among little girls that the arrests of females for this offence in 1855 reached an immense number of nearly 6000. I was touched deeply by the little stories of woe of these children.[15]

The reasons for Brace's particular interest in poor children are not difficult to understand, as the historian Robert Bremner explains: "Being more numerous than adults, especially in an era when large families were the rule, children formed the largest group in the ranks of poverty. Their sufferings were most grievous and their own responsibility for their condition least apparent." Improving their situation was also essential to the good of society as a whole.[16] Even as this book is written, children make up a disproportionate number of the American poor.[17]

The annual report of Children's Aid for 1858 noted that the ranks of poor children included "boot-blacks, match-sellers, apple-vendors, button-peddlers, baggage-carriers and those engaged in other petty pursuits." Horatio Alger popularized their lives in such novels as *Ragged Dick*, in which a "gentleman" asks "our hero" why he is so "ragged and dirty."

"They didn't have no wash-bowls at the hotel where I stopped," said Dick.

"What hotel did you stop at?"

"The Box Hotel."

"The Box Hotel?"

"Yes sir, I slept in a box on Spruce Street."[18]

This was typical, according to the organization's later records of the Newsboys' Lodging House, with accounts describing the face of poverty when America itself was poor: "Many of those who are regular lodgers would otherwise sleep in market-houses, hay barges, old cellars, open stairways, ash barrels, coal barrels or walk the streets at night." Their lives were brutal in other ways, as M. S. Beach, editor of the *New York Sun*, observed in 1860. "Newsboys, as a class, were hard characters," he wrote. "A few leaders were 'up to anything,' and those not strong enough to match them physically, paid tribute. Downright highway robberies, committed by these leaders on the smaller 'fry,' were of daily occurrence." A tally in 1852 found that the city's prisons held four thousand criminals under the age of twenty-one.[19]

There is no doubt that Brace, if inspired by idealism, also feared the prospect of civil unrest and an upending of the social order. A failure to convince the poor, including many who were new to the country, of the virtues and benefits of middle-class American behaviors would lead to frightening results, he believed. Brace specifically recalled New York's anti-conscription riot of 1863, during the Civil War—the same era portrayed in the Martin Scorsese film *Gangs of New York*. He described "passing down the Bowery, just as a mob was apparently beginning, in regard, I believe, to the draft troubles." Brace continued:

> From every one of the hundreds of lanes and alleys there swarmed a strange wild crowd—long-haired, excited men begrimed with toil, ragged figures who had been buried in cellars or dark dens, persons who might have been leaders of emeutes in Paris or Warsaw, young men and boys armed to the teeth, many women inflamed with excitement, creeping and murderous looking creatures with the sight of plunder in their eyes, a vast motley, ragged crowed but with a fierce passion beginning to blaze in their faces, as if that time had come when poverty was to get its fair share of the vast luxuries of the rich.[20]

Yet it would be facile to ascribe Brace's work—which had begun a decade before the draft riots—to sheer self-protection of his social class, or to dismiss it as what the sociologists Frances Fox Piven and Richard Cloward, a little more than a century later, would criticize as "regulating the poor."[21] Brace clearly acted on the belief that the values he himself

prized had served the country well and would do the same for any and
all who adopted them. His Methodist religion, to be sure, played a powerful role in his motivation to uplift the less fortunate, even the criminals
among them. He wrote:

> The spirit of Christ is slowly and irresistibly permeating even this
> lowest class of miserable, unfortunate, or criminal beings; inspiring
> those who perseveringly labor for them, drawing from wealth its
> dole and from intelligence its service of love, educating the fortunate
> in the habit of duty to the unfortunate, giving a dignity to the most
> degraded and offering hope to the despairing. CHRIST leads the
> Reform of the world, as well as its Charity.[22]

Though himself religiously inspired, Brace well understood that his
message needed a secular angle too, lest his target audience hear it as a
mere "Sunday School dodge." Indeed, his core theme was not religious;
it was not a message that would have come from the pulpit. It was not
about sin and salvation, but very much focused on the here-and-now,
on ways of thinking and specific positive steps that led to employment,
personal fulfillment, and perhaps even prosperity.

Brace was a missionary of bourgeois norms: education, thrift, marriage, and honesty. It was far from inevitable that these values would
become widespread American cultural norms. It would take the commitment of practical idealists to make it happen.

He first turned his attention to New York's legions of newsboys, who
were swarming the streets selling the tabloids of Pulitzer and Hearst, hoping each day for a headline that would attract buyers. Their bread-and-
butter was the *New York Sun*, the first city newspaper to feature stories of
crime and daily life (as well as a famous 1835 hoax about a civilization on
the moon). The *Sun* began the "penny press," and its business model was
based on street sales. It was thus not mere coincidence that Brace began
the work of his Children's Aid Society in space rented above the offices
of the *Sun*, at 125 Fulton Street in Lower Manhattan.

Seeing how many of the newsboys were homeless, "sleeping about in
boxes and alleyways," Brace understood that offering them shelter could
be the first step toward influencing them:

> It occurred to me that the best way of reaching them morally and mentally was by providing a comfortable shelter for them. I accordingly procured subscriptions from personal friends and through public meetings, and fitted up some rooms as a simple Lodging House.[23]

Brace recruited boys—and soon enough, girls also—to his lodging houses with the promise of a clean bed and a good meal. Significantly, they arrived voluntarily and could choose to leave. Thus, Brace had to create a setting and a message that they would freely embrace. His organization's 1861 annual report detailed what was on offer:

> The evenings of the week are passed variously by the boys. On Wednesday there is an interesting lecture; on Thursday a prayer meeting; on Friday a singing teacher attends; and on Sunday there are exercises appropriate to the Sabbath. The Afternoon and Evening School occupies the other evenings of the week, a brief devotional exercise meeting closing every day. The free Sunday dinner is still provided and given to all who refrain from working that day.

As the original Newsboys' Lodging House grew, it came to include a gym and a savings bank, "to induce the boys to save for they were great spendthrifts." Asked to contribute to the institution's operating expenses with their earnings (some contribution was required), the boys themselves helped support "a night school for instruction and a Sunday evening Religious meeting." While Brace served large numbers of people, he did not open the door to any and all: those over eighteen years of age were not to be admitted, lest they exert a bad influence on the younger people.

He wrote frankly about the difficulty of gaining the confidence of boys drawn in by a clean, warm bed, and turning their minds to higher values. After a Sunday sermon "putting forth vague and declamatory religious exhortation," the response was "'*Gas! gas!*' whispered with infinite contempt from one hard-faced young disciple to another." Brace might ask them, "My boys, what is the great end of man? When is he happiest? How would *you* feel happiest?" And their response would be: "When we'd plenty of hard cash, sir!"[24] Over time, Brace adjusted his tone to connect with his listeners such that they could relate.

Consider his sermon titled "Saving and Gambling," wherein he deftly acknowledges both envy and ambition, appealing to both in the service of his theme of thrift and steady personal improvement. His tone is high-minded and formal, respecting the intelligence of his audience; the language is clear and pointed:

> I understand very well the immense temptation which money is to each one of you boys. You know the value of gold as well as any merchant in Wall Street. A gentleman's son, who has his regular spending-money for luxuries, and who is always sure of his bed and his dinner, knows very little what money is to one of you. If he spends or loses a shilling, more or less, it makes very little difference to him. But with you, a shilling often determines whether you are to have a dinner or to go hungry; whether you are to sleep in a box, or on a bed....
>
> ...You understand how much running or shouting with your papers, or how many polishings of boots, must be gone through with, before a dollar is earned....
>
> Some of you imagine that if, in place of drudging away, day after day, earning a few shillings, you go down to a lottery-office and buy a "policy ticket," you can at once make a fortune....
>
> ...You take your pennies down to those cellars on N___ Street, and suppose, by cards or by dice, that you can save labor, and double or treble them easily.... You hope [those gambling salons] are the way to Fifth Avenue; but they are in fact the ferry to Blackwell's Island.... As very few gamblers ever win much money, they are constantly trying to make up their losses by dishonest means. They cheat even their comrades; they pilfer, they steal, they commit burglary, they rob on the high-way.[25]

Brace strove to impress upon the boys that gambling and dishonest dealing were not a reliable route to prosperity. The better alternative was honest hard work: "If you are selling papers, run fast and be quick, do honestly by every one who deals with you, work early and late, and you will soon begin to save money." Then they could earn interest on their savings in the bank provided by the lodging house. "That is the way many men acquire wealth—by constant saving and hard work," said Brace. "At any rate, whether you are rich or not, you make an honest living and you have no reason to be ashamed of your business, and no fear of the law." Brace cited Abraham Lincoln and John Jacob Astor, among others, as examples of men who "advanced by slow, steady steps," and he told the boys, "You can do the same. You may not reach as high, for you may not have as much talent; but you can, at least, win a respectable position for yourself."

Just as notable as what Brace did for the newsboys is what he did *not* do. In contrast to latter-day reformers, he did not wage a campaign against New York's newspapers for exploiting the newsboys, although such a case could plausibly have been made. He saw difficult, austere conditions as a fact of life, to be overcome through efforts toward personal advancement, not by a short-term amelioration of the conditions, nor by a challenge to the commercial system itself and the role of young newsboys in it. Brace's goal was to help individuals acquire the personal tools to prosper within the system.

The route to improvement for some, Brace believed, was to go west (as his New York contemporary Horace Greely put it). Children were sent on "orphan trains" to be placed in the household of an American farm family, in the expectation that all would benefit from the arrangement. "The United States have the enormous advantage over all other countries in the treatment of the difficult question of pauperism and reform, that they possess a practically unlimited area of arable land," wrote Brace. "The demand for labor on this land is beyond any present supply. Moreover, the cultivators of the soil are in America our most solid and intelligent class."[26] The children "placed out" were decidedly not to be viewed as servants, but as members of the family that took them in, sharing in their "social tone" and being "associates" of the family's own children.[27]

Brace applied his ideas in lodging houses and evening schools for the adolescent poor, in foster care and orphan trains. The scale of his undertaking might seem to border on the incredible, but there is no doubt that he built a child-saving colossus through his vision, language, values, and, not least, his fundraising prowess. Starting with a lone assistant in a rented loft above a newspaper office and preaching to newsboys who found the experience of a featherbed to be novel, he then succeeded in the crucial next step: convincing others, including many people with money, that his idea of social norms was the right idea *and that it should be assertively spread*.

Brace's approach can be described as "one size fits all," rooted in the belief that behavioral norms are universally appropriate. Today's professional social workers would not approve. For instance, Mark J. Stern and June Axinn write in their social work textbook, *Social Welfare: A History of the American Response to Need*, that Brace and those involved in "child-saving" efforts like his offered "mass, as opposed to individualized care, for children."[28] This is meant as criticism, implying a failure to recognize the different needs of individuals. The profession of social work had come to focus on the specific problems of a given family, and Brace's "one size fits all" method might seem primitive from this perspective. But for Brace and those influenced by him—including, decades later, the Juvenile Aid Society, which assisted my orphaned father—there were social and behavioral norms that everyone should strive to practice. That was the effective "policy" of the time, conceived and implemented by civil society.

By the time of Brace's death in 1890, his Children's Aid Society was running twenty-one industrial schools, thirteen night schools for general education, four summer camps, a typing school, a print shop, and three reading rooms, in addition to the lodging houses.[29] Between 1853 (the year of its founding) and 1893, the organization assisted a total of 85,000 children in its schools. But it was best known, and to some extent controversial, for the orphan trains: by the end of World War I, more than 120,000 poor children from New York had been "placed out" with farm families in the Midwest.[30] Just as importantly, Brace pointed the way for legions of successors to build charitable, civil society organizations with wide reach and influence. He created a blueprint for private nonprofits, for which leading citizens provided philanthropic support and volunteer leadership, accepting only limited government funding for specific purposes of their own conception, and giving careful scrutiny to the effectiveness of their methods.

A major reason for Brace's invitation to speak at the Harvard Divinity School in 1881, according to Charles Eliot, the president of Harvard, was to show the students "how a far-reaching and efficient charity was organized and how it does its work." In speaking of a "far-reaching" charity, Eliot no doubt meant that Brace didn't just serve legions of individuals directly, but also helped far more as the influence of his ideas spread, first by word of mouth in Manhattan's Lower East Side and then beyond. Brace himself expressed confidence that others would recognize the effectiveness of his method, with its emphasis on character and habits of life:

> The principal value of our Enterprise, we believe, as distinguished from similar efforts, is that our whole influence is *moral* and in no respect coercive. Those who have much to do with alms-giving and plans of human improvement soon see how superficial and comparatively useless all assistance or organization is which does not touch habits of life and the inner forces which form character.[31]

Brace thought hard about "habits of life" and how to influence them, but his aim was to inspire rather than correct. He did so with stories of men who "have given up everything for a cause, and got back nothing material," and stories about "the highest Sacrifice of all, where all was apparently lost and yet where all was gained." Sometimes the boys were warned against particular evils: "We preach on making false change, on selling old papers for new, on lying to employers, on stealing, fighting and gambling." But the goal transcended teaching specific rules of good behavior to boys who were "ignorant, homeless, with few high ideals," for they would go out again and "be exposed to every low, brutal and powerful temptation. They will be tempted, on the day after your meeting, to steal and fight, to get drunk and rob, to lie and swear and to indulge in every kind of vice." What they needed, Brace believed, was "some Power to hold them up against this torrent of temptation, something which will elevate and ennoble their nature, which will enable them to rise above the waves of vice and evil about them."[32] Whether Brace was referring to a religious power or simple self-discipline is unclear, but it's likely that he meant both.

The industrial schools for girls likewise put a premium on character development while offering what today we would call a job-training program, in sewing and other domestic arts. Brace recalled being shocked by the language of the little girls and the "pandemonium" in the schoolroom, but he noticed that the example of healthy norms slowly worked its effect:

> Yet the gradual effects of kindness, the influence of patience and of tact in discipline have steadily changed these schools into the most orderly and most industrious places of education in the city.... The

effect of the cleanliness and order enjoined, the influence of discipline and industry as well as the moral teachings given, were to raise these little girls above the reach of the usual feminine temptations of their class.[33]

While there were differences between the schools for girls and the programs for boys, the underlying principle was the same: setting norms for behavior to guide development into adult life.

Building support for his organization was also a process to which Brace gave careful thought. He had decided views, for instance, on recruiting a "suitable" board of trustees: they should be "not from the richest class alone, but from persons of middle fortune and moderate means," and most importantly they must be "of the highest character and responsibility." A type to be avoided was "the crotchety man with a bee in his bonnet, with a pet theory of reforming the world in ninety days which he forces in on all occasions." The Children's Aid Society was, after all, a practical undertaking with a multitude of tasks: raising operating funds, recruiting volunteers for the lodging houses and the industrial schools, selecting books for the reading rooms, finding "host" families in the West. For such purposes "you need men of pliability and good sense, who can work easily together and who will not let petty personal ends take the place of the great object they are promoting."[34]

Brace was similarly careful in hiring employees who exemplified the norms he espoused. Mr. and Mrs. Troll, "the superintendent and matron" of a girls' lodging house, "were well-fitted to the task and before long habits of personal cleanliness, early rising and going to bed at a regular hour were taught to the girls."[35] There was also "the superintendent at the house on Rivington Street, Mr. Calder," who had "shown taste and skill in making the house attractive to the children, and had a little greenhouse of his own."[36] Even the physical surroundings had a part in modeling norms.

In a time long before social service became a profession, Brace warned of the difference between careerism and calling. He considered it "of the utmost importance" that those who worked for his organization "should have their life and heart in their work, and should act as if it were their own." All of those who labor in a charitable organization "should have a deep moral interest in it, and not a mere professional part." Hiring on the basis of genuine commitment to the organization's goals allowed him to assert that "during twenty-three years, over three millions of dollars have passed through the hands of the employees and so far as is known, not a dollar was ever stolen or wasted."[37]

When it came to fundraising, Brace also had strong opinions. Just as he urged adolescents to avoid shortcuts to wealth, he turned down offers by celebrities (for example, "a benevolent prize-fighter") to stage benefits for the Children's Aid Society. The cause must speak for itself, he believed; it must appeal to the public on its own terms. "The true and manly course for a charity is to show everyone what you are doing, to make people familiar with the classes you labor for and the evils you seek to cure; to give the utmost publicity to all these benevolent efforts, and to cause the public to feel that the charity belongs to them and must be supported by them." In fact, Children's Aid turned out to be a prodigious fundraising enterprise, drawing "gifts and subscriptions from every part of the United States."[38] Brace, in effect, was writing the playbook for private charitable fundraising, and his market analysis has not expired with age.

He noted that the United States had some very wealthy individuals, many of them with a desire to channel their wealth to worthy purposes: "There is now in this country a great amount of wealth accumulation in the hands of persons who do not care to found families, but are anxious to found charities, endow colleges, build institutions of benevolence and otherwise promote the public welfare by generous benefactions."[39] In 1881, such contributions brought in some $225,000—the equivalent of more than $5 million in 2018 dollars. That Brace could raise money in such impressive amounts tells a story in itself: whether he had tapped into norms already embraced by many other Americans, or had convinced them that the norms he was espousing were of the right sort, he was leading a crusade with a multitude of willing followers.

In *The Dangerous Classes,* he thanks specific wealthy donors who helped the Children's Aid Society create an endowment. There was one Chauncy Rose, inheritor of a million-dollar estate, who "with a rare conscience and generosity, felt it his duty not to use any of this large estate for himself. To our Society he gave something like $200,000. Of this we made $150,000 an invested fund." Donations came from people with old New York names such as Stuyvesant, Astor, and Van Rensselaer, but many more arrived from people of apparently modest means: an "account carpenter" contributed $2, for example, and a "collection in Congregational Church, Orwell, Ohio," yielded $4.79. Brace had made uplifting New York's impoverished children a national concern, and he thought it good that current donations were covering a substantial proportion of necessary expenses, "so that the Society might have the vitality arising from constant contact with the public."[40]

Children's Aid, it must be acknowledged, did not rely solely on private contributions. Brace recorded, for example, that of the $200,000 received in 1870 (which included $32,000 to purchase two lodging houses), some $60,000 had come from county taxes and nearly $20,000 from the city board of education, "being a *pro rata* allotment on the average number of pupils."[41] The public purse, in other words, was helping to defray the cost of the organization's schools. But crucially, the schools do not appear to have been founded with an expectation of such assistance; they were conceived by Brace himself, not by the public authorities. Public funds, however, allowed him to perform more of the kind of charity he envisioned in the first place.

This balance between private contributions and public funding would change dramatically in the mid-twentieth century with the rise of the "nonprofit" state, which now provides the overwhelming share of funding for social service organizations, whose activities are directed by detailed contracts. Examples include the present-day Children's Aid Society, which continues in a form that Brace would likely not have imagined. In 2015 it received some $80 million in government grants, along with only $17 million in private contributions.[42]

Considering Brace's success in raising funds, it bears reiterating that his Children's Aid Society was a departure from historical precedent. While it could be described as "faith-inspired," it was not a religious organization, nor was it a puppet of a church or synagogue. Neither was it an arm of government. It was a new hybrid organization of a type that would prove to have staying power in American society. But as a novelty, receiving no small amount of public funds, it raised controversy in its day. There was friction with other types of institutions, particularly the Catholic Church. When one is in the norm-setting business, after all, one risks conflict with those who have other ideas.

Traditionally, each religious group cared for its own, whereas Brace—

though a Methodist minister himself—believed that his organization's aims and its governing board should be nonsectarian. "We have in our schools, Jews, Quakers and Agnostics working with others to aid the poor. In our Board of Trustees there have been for twenty-five years men of all kinds of belief, and there has never been the slightest friction or trouble from this source among them."[43] But Catholics presented a theological challenge and a source of tension for Brace. Although he praised Irish priests for urging temperance and wrote positively of his meetings with Catholic clergy in Europe, he also criticized the "spiritual lifelessness of Romanism" and its "chilling formalism," and there is little doubt that he was disdainful of the Catholic Church in New York. He insisted that he had no interest in proselytizing, yet the Church could not help but notice that he was indirectly bringing a form of the Protestant gospel of self-improvement (even if its religious aspect was de-emphasized) to children of Irish, Italian, and German Catholic immigrants.

As a result, Brace did not have a clear and easy path on which to proceed. When he opened a school for the children of Italian immigrants in Manhattan's infamous Five Points slum, attendance was robust at first, but quickly declined. "Some absurd rumors had been circulated among them to the effect that our purpose was to turn them away from their own church," Brace discovered.[44] The Church also objected to the placing out of Catholic orphans (or even so-called "half-orphans") with farm families. Brace complained that the Catholic poor "were early taught, even from the altar, that the whole scheme of emigration was one of 'proselytizing,' and that every child thus taken forth was made a 'Protestant.'"[45] He contended that this charge was untrue, and that "Catholic and Protestant homes were offered freely to the children. No child's creed was interfered with."[46] Brace was frustrated by resistance and competition from Catholics: "A class of children, whom we used thus to benefit, are now sent to the Catholic Protectory," or kept in the city almshouse. "Were our movement allowed its full scope," he said, "we could take the place of every Orphan Asylum and Alms-house for pauper children in and around New York, and thus save the public hundreds of thousands of dollars."[47]

Of course, the Catholic Church would have had every incentive to oppose sending thousands of members of its future generation to an uncertain religious fate. On a more practical level, the Church had good reason to resent Brace for lining up government assistance for his schools, given that New York state law since 1844 explicitly banned state aid for parochial school education. Brace may not have viewed his lodging houses and schools as religious institutions, and clearly he convinced the authorities that they were not. Even so, as the sociologist Andrew Polsky has observed in his historical overview of the American social service system, the idea of "individual moral responsibility" is "deeply embedded in our liberal Protestant culture."[48]

Evaluating the work of Brace and his Children's Aid Society cannot be based on his good intentions alone, of course. Brace himself was alive to the need to offer evidence of success, and in his 1881 Harvard address he cited some encouraging New York police data: "The commitments of girls and women for vagrancy fell off from 5,880 in 1860, to 2,045 in 1879, or from 1 in every 138$\frac{1}{2}$ persons in 1860 (when the population was 864,224) to 1 in every 536$\frac{1}{2}$ in 1879 (when the population was 1,079,563)." He concluded, "This certainly looks like some effect from reformatory efforts."[49]Assigning credit to the Children's Aid Society may be a reach, but it is not implausible. After all, it is likely that the enterprise influenced not only those it touched directly, but many others who were inspired by a good example as it spread outward. That is how positive cultural norms work in practice.

The Children's Aid Society could also boast of testimonials from outside observers. One "W. H. Lefferts, Sergt. D. A. Police" sent a letter in 1861 reporting that "there are not one half as many petty thieves and female offenders against property, as last year, or in former years."[50] M. S. Beach, the editor of the *Sun*, was more explicit in giving credit to the Newsboys' Lodging House. In contrast to previous years, he wrote, "a fight or a row among the newsboys is seldom seen. The smaller ones pursue their traffic unmolested and all things relating to the newsboys give token of better times among them. If these changes are not all due to the Lodging House, I believe that by far the greater part of them can be traced directly to that as the cause."[51] A letter from one of the newspaper's business managers remarked that "the newsboys of the present day may be said to be an entirely different class" from those of earlier days.[52]

Brace offered a more direct, if somewhat limited, measure of effectiveness when it came to his orphan trains. In his 1881 speech, he told of tracking forty-five children ("selected at random") who had all been sent west on a single rail line, the Michigan Central. The thirty-four he could locate "had all done well with one exception," he said. "They had earned property; some received good salaries; some were in professions, most were married, and were respected in their communities." The one exception had cheated his employer after he had grown to manhood.

Some of those who were sent west or were alumni of a lodging house took the time later in life to write to the Children's Aid Society, with words of inspiration. Brace quoted one such letter to the superintendent of the Newsboys' Lodging House:

> All the newsboys of New York have a bad name; but we should show
> ...that we are no fools; that we can become as respectable as any of
> their countrymen, for some of you poor boys can do something for
> your country—for Franklin, Webster, Clay, were poor boys once,
> and even...Vanderbilt, and Astor....So now, boys, stand up and let
> them see you have got the real stuff in you. Come out here and make
> respectable and honorable men, so they can say, there, that boy was
> once a newsboy.[53]

Such letters may have been exactly the sort of tribute that Brace himself most desired.

Upon his death in August 1890 (during a visit to Switzerland), Brace was widely eulogized for the qualities that equipped him to build an organization on his own terms. Wrote the *New York Evening Post*, "He had every quality for philanthropic work; clear insight, perfect sanity of judgment, supreme diligence and indomitable patience."[54] His daughter cited another newspaper tribute (though she did not specify the source): "The death of no citizen of this municipality could bring a sense of personal loss and grief to so many of its inhabitants, as that of Charles Loring Brace."[55]

A memorial service for Brace was held in the Newsboys' Lodging House.

# 2

# JANE ADDAMS: FROM NORMS TO REFORM

Not all of the poor in America in the nineteenth and early twentieth centuries were children, of course. The cities of the East and the industrial Midwest were swelling with vast numbers of poor immigrant families from central and eastern Europe, many of whom were unacquainted with such concepts as citizenship in a democracy. Steps were taken to familiarize them with the norms for successful integration into American life. In 1892, for instance, the popular Boston-based magazine *The Youth's Companion* first published the Pledge of Allegiance, written by its staff member Francis Bellamy, combining a salute to the American flag with the promise of "liberty and justice for all." (Notwithstanding its name, the magazine published some content for adults, including the writing of Jack London, Willa Cather, and Harriet Beecher Stowe.) Around the same time, the daughter of a wealthy small-town mill owner and railroad investor moved to Chicago's West Side and began a mission to teach the values of citizenship to new immigrants.

Born in 1860, Jane Addams was raised in Cedarville, Illinois, on prairie surrounded by hills. One of those hills, she wrote, was "crowned by pine woods, grown up from a bag full of Norway pine seeds sown by my father the very year he came to Illinois, testimony perhaps that the most vigorous pioneers gave at least an occasional thought to beauty."[1]

Her parents, John and Sarah, had come from Pennsylvania to Cedar-ville in 1844, purchasing and expanding a flour mill on Cedar Creek. Eventually they owned a prosperous complex including mills for flour, linseed, and lumber. John also invested successfully in railroads, found-ed a major insurance company and a bank, and built a Federal-style mansion for his family. Jane was the eighth of nine children, of whom only four survived.

The Addams family traced their roots in America to recipients of land grants from William Penn, and some family members had fought in the Revolutionary War. John Addams was a Hicksite Quaker, believ-ing more in guidance by an "inward light" than the biblical authority that more orthodox Quakers followed. A civic-spirited man who served eight terms in the Illinois Senate, he was a contemporary and friend of Abraham Lincoln and among the founders of the Republican Party. (He helped bring the second Lincoln-Douglas debate to nearby Freeport.) Lincoln corresponded regularly with Addams—in one letter expressing confidence that "Mr. Dear Double D Addams" would "vote according to his conscience," but begging to know in which direction that conscience "was pointing." Jane remembered seeing her father in tears for the first time on the day he learned that Lincoln was dead.

Jane was close to her father, especially in her early years after her mother had died and her father had not yet remarried. In her classic memoir, *Twenty Years at Hull-House*, she recalled formative moments with the father she admired as a "self-made man," who all his life con-tinued to rise at 3 a.m. just as when he was a young apprentice learning the mill business in Pennsylvania. As the family grew wealthy, Jane told herself that she must do more with her life than simply live on her inher-itance. That her calling would be the uplift of the immigrant poor is not altogether surprising given her childhood memories of learning about poverty and inequality.

As a seven-year-old girl, for example, she accompanied her father on a visit to a mill in the neighboring town, adjacent to its poorest quarter. She vividly recalled what she saw that day and how it affected her:

> Before then I had always seen the little city of ten thousand people
> with the admiring eyes of a country child, and it had never occurred
> to me that all its streets were not as bewilderingly attractive as the one

which contained the glittering toyshop and the confectioner. On that day, I had my first sight of the poverty which implies squalor....I remember launching at my father the pertinent inquiry why people lived in such horrid little houses so close together and...declared with much firmness when I grew up, I should, of course, have a large house, but it would not be built among the other large houses, but right in the midst of horrid houses like those.[2]

And so began the idea of mingling her life with those of the less well-off. Eventually she would establish an institution where she lived in a mansion surrounded by ten other community buildings among the little houses of Chicago's Near West Side.

Another formative incident occurred when she was eight years old and preparing to set out for Sunday School. "Arrayed in a new cloak, gorgeous beyond anything I had ever worn before, I stood before my father for approval," she recalled. He agreed that the cloak was very pretty, but advised that she wear her old cloak instead, for it would keep her "quite as warm, with the added advantage of not making the other little girls feel badly." The exchange prompted young Jane to ponder "the old question eternally suggested by the inequalities of the human lot." Continuing her story, she wrote: "Only as we neared the church door did I venture to ask what could be done about it, receiving the reply that it might never be righted so far as clothes went, but that people might be equal in things that mattered more than clothes, the affairs of education and religion, for instance."[3]

Jane herself was educated at the Rockford Female Seminary, later Rockford College (the same sort of school for women that the Brace family had founded). Harboring since girlhood "a curious sense of responsibility for carrying on the world's affairs," she eventually found her true calling when she came to Chicago in 1889 with Ellen Gates Starr, a friend who had been her traveling companion in Europe. They brought with them a model for assisting the poor that they had seen in London. Toynbee Hall was the first institution to call itself a "settlement house": a residence in a poor or immigrant neighborhood where people from well-to-do backgrounds would literally "settle," living among the less fortunate and helping them adjust to urban life in an industrial economy.

Addams, like Charles Loring Brace, was motivated in no small part by religious belief, though of an ecumenical sort. "Other motives which make toward the Settlement are the result of a certain renaissance going forward in Christianity," she wrote. "The impulse to share the lives of the poor, the desire to make social service, irrespective of propaganda, express the spirit of Christ, is as old as Christianity itself."[4] The influential institution she founded was, like the Children's Aid Society, essentially Christian in spirit but nondenominational in form. It would not be an arm of church or government, but a product of civil society, and in that respect it was quintessentially American.

Settlement houses were envisioned as a means to bring the affluent and the poor in contact by attracting idealistic, upper-middle-class youths of college age into poor neighborhoods. Addams became known as "head resident" of Hull House (in the former mansion of one Charles Hull), and she identified with all the potential settlement volunteers whose sense of "uselessness hangs heavily upon them" and who sought an outlet for their idealism. In other words, the benefits of this initiative would not flow in one direction only. But the settlement pioneers did not hesitate to express a belief that the poor would gain from proximity with the better-off. There would be a kind of equalizing effect, as Addams explained in a paper for the American Academy of Social Science in 1899: "The American settlement has represented not so much a sense of duty of the privileged toward the unprivileged . . . as a desire to *equalize through social effort* those results which superior opportunity may have given the possessor." (Emphasis added.)[5]

As abstract as that formulation sounds, Addams built an institution that might today be called a community center, dealing with the most practical matters facing the amazing range of immigrant families who crowded into the apartment buildings surrounding the Hull mansion— Irish, Italian, Jewish, Greek, Polish, and more. It began with the smallest steps: a reading room and personal invitations to neighborhood mothers to join Addams and Ellen Starr for dinner. The offerings expanded quickly and dramatically. Many neighborhood residents who had previously lacked opportunities for education and recreation here found "kindergarten classes, an adult night school, various social clubs for older children, a public kitchen, a gym, a theater, a music school, a swimming pool, a library, an employment bureau and even an art gallery."⁶ In fact, the first major charitable contribution to augment Addams's personal seed money came from a Chicagoan who responded to Starr's appeal for funds to open the gallery. It immediately proved even more popular with the neighborhood than a pantry offering what Addams thought to be healthy foods at low prices.

Within a decade, Hull House was a major institution, well known in Chicago and around the United States. It would figure importantly in any number of nearly incredible stories, including that of Benny Goodman, the "King of Swing," who learned to play the clarinet at Hull House and returned regularly to perform there, even at the height of his fame. Decades later, the playwright David Mamet got his start at Hull-House Theatre.

Like Brace, Addams created an attractive setting and message that neighborhood residents sought out of their own volition. Also like Brace, she built an institution based on her own ideas—and with private support garnered through social circles. Hull House was far more than a neighborhood recreation center. There is no doubt that what became an impressive physical facility also served as a vehicle for promoting social norms—offered not in the spirit of correction or reprimand but as part of the acculturation that would help the poor improve their condition, which was understood to be their own goal.

In *Twenty Years at Hull-House*, Addams recalled her early impressions of a neighborhood where much needed to be improved, beginning with sanitation:

> [T]he immigrant population, nine tenths of them from the country, . . . carried on all sorts of traditional activities in the crowded tenements. That a group of Greeks should be permitted to slaughter sheep in a basement, that Italian women should be allowed to sort over rags collected from the city dumps . . . in a court swarming with children, that immigrant bakers should continue unmolested to bake their bread for their neighbors in unspeakably filthy spaces under the pavement, appeared incredible to visitors accustomed to careful city regulations.

It was her hope that city regulations might not be enforced against some of these activities, but she firmly believed that the immigrant poor should adjust to the standards of their new home.

As garbage filled the alleys and tuberculosis bacteria (a.k.a. the "white hearse") filled the air, Addams waged a clean-up campaign:

> We [at Hull House] arranged many talks for the immigrants, point- ing out that although a woman may sweep her own doorway in her native village and allow the refuse to innocently decay in the open air and sunshine, in a crowded city quarter, if the garbage is not prop- erly collected and destroyed, a tenement-house mother may see her children sicken and die, and that the immigrants must therefore not only keep their own houses clean, but must also help the authorities to keep the city clean.[7]

The immigrants learned that the proper disposal of garbage was not just in their own interest, but also a responsibility of good citizenship.

Addams did not rely on talk alone to promote the value of cleanliness. She used more creative means as well, including a May Day celebration with a Maypole dance and a May Queen, held on a playground that Hull House had built:

> I remember that one year that honor of being queen was offered to the little girl who should pick up the largest number of scraps of paper which littered all the streets and alleys. The children that spring had been organized into a league, and each member had been provided with a stiff piece of wire upon the sharpened point of which stray bits of paper were impaled and later soberly counted off into a large box in the Hull-House alley. The little Italian girl who thus won the scepter took it very gravely as the just reward of hard labor, and we were all so absorbed in the desire for clean and tidy streets that we were wholly oblivious to the incongruity of thus selecting "the queen of love and beauty."[8]

Yet Addams realized that she was, in an important way, promoting the norms of love and beauty—and was glad of it.

Addams was by no means aiming to Americanize immigrants at the cost of their own native culture. She celebrated the way that Italian and Bohemian peasants living in Chicago "still put on their bright holiday clothes on a Sunday and go to visit their cousins. They tramp along with at least a suggestion of having once walked over plowed fields and breathed country air."[9] Indeed, she feared that the son of an immigrant father "laughed loud at him" for his traditional habits but would enjoy no "pastoral interlude" himself. Still, she was unabashed about her goal of exposing those children to the norms appropriate to their new surroundings. "One thing seemed clear in regard to entertaining immigrants," she wrote: "to preserve and keep whatever of value their past life contained and to bring them in contact with a better type of Americans."[10]

The influence of Addams and Hull House extended far beyond the Near West Side, and far beyond Chicago, for that matter. This reach must be credited, in part, to the fact that its leaders were well-educated, affluent women, as well as avowed feminists in an era before women's suffrage. Most, including Addams, were unmarried, and at first there was a sense of novelty about their role. But Addams and her counterparts in other cities—especially Lillian Wald, the founder of the Henry Street Settlement in New York—quickly became widely admired public figures.

Indeed, the acclaim won by Hull House sparked a movement that extended across the country—and across the racial divide—well before the age of federal government programs and grants. In 1913, the *Handbook of Settlements* (by Robert Woods and Albert Kennedy, founders of Boston's South End House) listed no fewer than 413 organizations similar to Hull House.[11] Typically they combined attractive facilities such as a gym and a pool with initiatives clearly aimed at acculturating the urban poor to what can only be called bourgeois norms.

There was Lowell House in New Haven, located in "a factory district" populated by "Jews, Russians, Germans," and offering amenities such as "noon lunch club for factory girls, piano lessons and practice, branch of the public library, a bank, classes in painting, iron work, dressmaking; English classes for foreigners." Cleveland's Alta House, founded and financed by no less a personage than John D. Rockefeller (who started the Standard Oil Company in Cleveland) aimed "to help to educate the children mentally, morally, and physically, and through them to aid in every effort to elevate and purify home life and the life of the neighborhood," which was "an Italian community of about ten thousand people."

It had a resident staff of ten women and six men. Pittsburgh's Kingsley House, like many settlements, maintained an extensive "summer plant," including "an eighty-nine acre farm" along with "a central building and six wings, 4 cottages, barns, tents; a specially built cement swimming pool, etc., etc."

The "summer home" is a tradition that Charles Loring Brace had helped establish. In his 1884 address to the National Conference of Charities and Correction in St. Louis, he described the summer home that the Children's Aid Society created in then-rural Bath, Long Island, which was visited each summer by some four thousand poor city children: "Here they enjoy, for the first time, clean beds, nourishing fare and pure air from the great ocean." The experience was an "initiation" for the children in "the first lessons of civilization," as many of them "have never slept 'between two sheets'; . . . many have not had a 'square meal' and evidently do not know the use of the knife and fork." This introduction to middle-class social graces included what Brace called the "doctrine of oatmeal." He reported that the children "did not at first relish oatmeal and good milk for breakfast, but much preferred their usual ration of coffee with a little hot bread. Great numbers however acquired a taste for this nutritious food, and have induced their mothers to cook it."[12] The Long Island summer home was the result of a $20,000 gift from a single donor (nearly half a million in 2018 dollars).

Private philanthropy was the exclusive source of financial support for the settlements as well—and was not to be taken for granted. Addams, like Brace, founded a nonprofit entity, the Hull House Association, to enlist, most notably, young women from well-off families. The contributions of an heiress named Mary Smith were credited with the "overcoming of deficits here and there, small but apparently unsurmountable, that literally kept the work going, or at any rate kept Jane Addams from black discouragement."[13] Addams herself raised funds through speaking fees. (Of course, budget pressure reflected the success of her ambition to expand the scope of her efforts.) Other major settlements cultivated deep community pockets, as well as relying on individual philanthropy. Lillian Wald's Henry Street Settlement in New York depended heavily on Jacob Schiff, a financier who contributed secretly to support a fellow German Jew in her work to Americanize eastern European Jews. Kingsley House in Pittsburgh developed an endowment based on the gifts of more than nine hundred individual donors. Results bordered on the spectacular. In 1909 alone, its "summer plant" hosted some 3,838 guests—in the service of "social intercourse, mutual helpfulness, mental and moral improvement, and rational and healthful recreation."[14]

The influence of such approaches extended beyond the organizations that defined themselves strictly as settlement houses. Philadelphia's Juvenile Aid Society—the group that assisted my father—had started as a "child-saving" organization very much in the Children's Aid Society mold, "placing" orphans and others from troubled families in healthful foster homes. But by the time it was looking out for my father, it offered such additional programs as medical and dental clinics, and several weeks at a summer camp where cabins were named for local colleges. It was there that my father developed a fascination with astronomy, seeing stars he'd never seen in South Philadelphia. (His nickname became Jupiter— both for the planet and for the Mozart symphony.) What had begun strictly as a "child-saving" organization had evolved into something much bigger. Indeed, one can think of private social service generally as a series of new stories built upon a modest foundation.

Today, a member of the economic elite such as Jane Addams who seeks to improve the habits of the poor might be charged with condescension. But the residents of settlement houses recognized the drive for a better life in those they sought to uplift, and they understood the importance of encouraging upward mobility. At Henry Street, Lillian Wald—second only to Addams in renown as a settlement leader—marveled at the ambition she regularly encountered in the tenements of the Lower East Side, and especially the hopes for the next generation: "The passion of the Russian Jews for intellectual attainment recalls the spirit of the early New England families. . . . Here we are often witnesses of long-continued deprivation on the part of every member of the family [so] that there be a doctor, lawyer or teacher among them." One mother told her, "We do not expect things for ourselves. It is the chance for the children, education and freedom for them."[15]

It would be a blinkered historical account indeed that discounted the self-help efforts of immigrant groups: their credit unions and burial societies and religion-based homes for orphans. (My father used to joke about his neighborhood baseball team: the Chevre Kedisha White Sox, named after the Yiddish term for a burial society, such as the one to which his own father had belonged.) But it would also be wrong to discount the efforts of the American-born elites who took it upon themselves to assist the immigrant and native-born poor in assimilation and self-improvement. Henry Street provided lessons in how to live a life up from poverty. For instance, it maintained a Housekeeping Center, which Wald described in her own memoir, *The House on Henry Street*:

> A house was rented in a typical Henry Street tenement. Intelligence and taste were exercised in equipping it inexpensively and with furniture that required the least possible labor to keep it free of dirt and vermin. Classes were formed to teach housekeeping in its every detail, using nothing the people themselves could not procure.... Cleaning, disinfecting, actual purchasing of supplies in the shops of the neighborhood, household accounts, nursing, all the elements of homekeeping were systematically taught.
>
> The first winter that the Center was opened, the entire class consisted of girls engaged to be married—clerks, stenographers, teachers. None were prepared and all were eager to have the homes they were about to establish better organized and more intelligently conducted than those from which they had come.[16]

All who attended these classes did so voluntarily, not in exchange for monetary assistance but because they understood that the instruction offered was in their interest. One cannot, of course, fail to note that the classes were confined to young women about to be married. Wald did not stipulate that such a prospect was a requirement, nor is there discussion of whether the class would have excluded the unmarried mother if one were to have come forward. Nonetheless, it is hard to avoid concluding that such classes reinforced the norm of marriage—and just as important, its practical realities.

Both the zeal and the methods of Addams and Wald were shared by a much less known but just as noteworthy group: the African American women who took up the settlement house mission. The 413 organizations listed in the *Handbook of Settlements* overwhelmingly dealt with neighborhoods of European immigrants, but the movement also included similar efforts by American blacks. Margaret Washington, wife of the Tuskegee Institute's founder, Booker T. Washington—the most prominent African

American leader of his time—founded the Elizabeth Russell Settlement in Tuskegee, Alabama, in 1897. Unlike most settlements, it focused on a rural population, aiming "to better family conditions of the colored people on the plantation in the matter of cleanliness, education, uprightness—to teach them how to live." Maintained by "personal effort" and "occasional donations from Northern friends," it offered classes in sewing, cooking and agriculture.

The overwhelming majority of black settlement houses were established in cities to which rural blacks were beginning to move, in both the South and the North. In a part of Hampton, Virginia, inhabited mostly by African Americans, Mrs. Janie Porter Barrett established the Locust Street Settlement, run by sixteen women and four men volunteers. It offered a playground and a library, and sought to teach people "how to have more attractive homes, cleaner back yards, more attractive front yards, cleaner sidewalks," and "the proper food for the family."[17]

By one account, there were some seventy-two organizations that qualified as "Social Settlements for Negroes," found in virtually all states with sizeable black populations.[18] They were complemented by the work of the National Urban League, later known for its leadership in the civil rights movement, but established in part to help rural blacks adjust to urban life. (Its full name was the National Urban League for Social Service Among Negroes.)

A notable example of such organizations is the Neighborhood Union in Atlanta, founded by Lugenia Burns Hope, wife of John Hope, the president of Atlanta's historically black Morehead College. Her efforts and those of others like her represented an amazing leap of faith—the belief that self-improvement was worthwhile, notwithstanding the physical conditions of black neighborhoods and the legal strictures of Jim Crow segregation. The neighborhood of Summerhill in the southeast of Atlanta, for example, was one in which "the Black residents owned small pieces of unimproved property" as well as "homes and businesses," but they were "not able to get lights, water, sewage disposal or pavement." Even in these circumstances, Burns believed in the value of improving moral conditions. She and others "succeeded in getting two families out of [the] district who indulged in doing things that were immoral such as breaking the Sabbath and gambling."[19] The Neighborhood Union built recreation facilities and health centers. Volunteer nurses and doctors made 135 home visits in July 1910 alone, as part of a campaign against tuberculosis and for better prenatal care.

Like the broader settlement house movement, these efforts by a black elite were designed to uplift the poor by proselytizing the message of social norms. The educated, middle-class women leading the initiatives were "Victorian in beliefs and values," notes Jacqueline Rouse. "They believed that the uplift of the race was intrinsically bound to 'moral uplift.'"[20] Members of the Neighborhood Union "believed that poverty and the lack of proper instruction and supervision were factors that led young people to pursue lives of crime," and therefore they "concentrated on 'capturing' young adults before they became victims of vice."[21] They regarded the heart of their task as teaching "refinement, culture, self-esteem, self-control, manners, morals, and high character," not just through the written text, but also by example.[22]

Efforts to shape social norms during the early twentieth century were not focused exclusively on the poor. This was a time when Boy Scouts, Girl Scouts, and 4-H Clubs (representing head, heart, hands, and health) were springing up nationwide—all emphasizing the formative. The YMCA, although founded in the 1850s as an evangelical Christian organization, became interdenominational, with an emphasis on morality and good citizenship. (It was in YMCA gyms that basketball and volleyball were invented.) Members of the Girl Scouts pledged, "On my honor, I will try: To serve God and my country, To help people at all times." Youth living on farms and in small towns who joined 4-H recited their own pledge: "I pledge my head to clearer thinking, my heart to greater loyalty, my hands to larger service, and my health to better living, for my club, my community, my country, and my world."

The idea that ambitious private organizations were needed to promote the norms of a healthy society was so ascendant that the Scouts and 4-H were granted unusual national charters by Congress, allowing them to operate as nonprofit, tax-exempt organizations in all fifty states. In signing the legislation to aid the Boy Scouts in 1916, President Woodrow Wilson said, "Anything that is done to increase the effectiveness of the Boy Scouts of America will be a genuine contribution to the welfare of the nation." Although the legislation didn't dispense public funding to the Boy Scouts, it was an important seal of approval—an official endorsement of bourgeois norms from the highest office in the United States.

Meanwhile, however, the settlement house movement began to change, expanding beyond the modeling and promotion of social norms. Neither Lugenia Hope Burns nor Jane Addams nor Lillian Wald nor the legions listed in the *Handbook of Settlements* limited themselves to teaching constructive behavior. They became political reformers, concerned with the means by which the government could improve conditions for the residents of the neighborhoods in which they worked.

The Atlanta Neighborhood Union, for example, pressured the city government to pave muddy streets and improve black schools. As early as 1908, the Union "began confronting the city of Atlanta with the urgent needs it was uncovering," and went to court with demands for "better health and housing programs, better streets and more streetlights to prevent crime."[23] While Jane Addams urged residents to clean up trash, she also secured a city appointment as the neighborhood "garbage inspector" and sought to improve trash pickup. Previously, that position had been more of a political reward than part of a serious sanitation effort. Over time, settlement leaders looked well beyond their neighborhood boundaries, envisioning and working toward policy prescriptions to improve the lives of their neighbors through "wholesale reform," and extending their reform focus nationwide.

Lillian Wald led a campaign to guarantee clean milk in New York— which entailed an understanding of the entire dairy supply chain. Jane Addams led a group of settlement residents turned reformers in campaigns for a wide range of social legislation: legal protections for garment workers, a minimum wage, limits on working hours, and protections for immigrants. Addams became a thorn in the side of the Chicago business establishment, urging department stores to reject clothing produced by "sweated" labor. (Her Hull House colleague Florence Kelley would found the National Consumers League, which organized boycotts of such products.) In 1892, reformers began investigating "sweat-shops" and campaigned for legislation on factory conditions and child labor. In response, department store advertisers ordered "thumbs down on those damned women."[24]

This was the start of Progressive-era reform, linking Addams with Lincoln Steffens and his "Shame of the Cities" journalism and even with the socialist Eugene Debs, who was sheltered by a Hull House associate when he was a wanted man during the bitter Pullman railroad strike of

1894 (and later bailed out of jail by Florence Kelley). George Pullman was considered a model employer in many ways, but Addams objected to the paternalism of his company town. She placed the greatest importance on preparing workers to do things for themselves, but also looked to government for reform laws so the working poor needn't depend on the benevolence of individuals.

By 1913, virtually all the settlements in the Woods and Kennedy handbook listed improvement of housing conditions as part of their mission. This Progressive zeal laid the groundwork for private, limited-profit "model tenements" and later for public housing, envisioned as a safe and sanitary replacement for slums. It's important to note that Jane Addams and Ellen Starr did not go into their work in the spirit of reformers or providers. Rather, they aimed to create a beneficial environment, "to make a place, if they could, in and around which a fuller life might grow, for others and for themselves, a happier life, a life richer in interest."[25] Nonetheless, even as Hull House continued to offer programs that helped immigrants and their children assimilate, Addams and her acolytes would play a key role in the establishment and expansion of social services under government direction.

A truly "remarkable group of women" lived and worked at Hull House during its early years, including Florence Kelley, Alice Hamilton, and Julia Lathrop.[26] Kelley, a Pennsylvania-born daughter of a Quaker abolitionist and Philadelphia congressman, would go on to be a cofounder of the National Association for the Advancement of Colored People, as well as the first general secretary of the National Consumers League. Hamilton was a physician (hardly commonplace for a woman at the time) who led investigations into occupation-related illnesses and helped establish the discipline of "industrial medicine." She later recalled her time at Hull House as deeply gratifying: "The life there satisfied every longing—for companionship, for the excitement of new experiences, for constant intellectual stimulation and for the sense of being caught up in a big movement which enlisted my enthusiastic loyalty."[27] Lathrop would be the first woman ever named to the Illinois State Board of Charities, and she joined with Kelley to press for the establishment of a federal Children's Bureau to serve as a "source of authoritative information about the welfare of children and their families."[28] Its most important leader would be another Hull House alumna, Grace Abbott.

The reform focus of these women would, like so many settlement innovations, filter through the social service world. At the Juvenile Aid Society (which took up the case of my father), the minutes of monthly meetings show regular contributions to the American Association for Labor Legislation, founded to advance social insurance programs such as the one that developed into Social Security.

Jane Addams became the reigning female symbol of political Progressivism, and by some accounts the most famous woman in America in the decade before World War I. She electrified the national Progressive Party convention that nominated Theodore Roosevelt in 1912 by being the first woman to second the nomination of a major presidential candidate. That same year, Addams was elected to lead the National Conference of Charities and Correction. The group's platform called for:

> a living wage; the regulation of hours of work; standards of sanitation and safety including compensation for injury and prohibition of manufacture of poisonous articles dangerous to the life of workers; the right to a home, safe and sanitary in healthful surroundings, with abolition of home [based] work and tenement manufacture; the regulation of the term of the working life, bounded by a minimum age to protect against child labor and a maximum age to insure the wage earner a time of economic independence from daily toil; and compensation against heavy loss sustained by industrial workers as a result of unavoidable accidents, industrial disease, sickness, unemployment, and old age.[29]

This platform would be the backbone of the liberal social welfare agenda of the twentieth century. Addams herself, once religiously inspired, became an agnostic and discontinued prayer services at Hull House. In essence, she became the original secular Progressive. Her emphasis had changed, to say the least.

The reform agenda that Addams promoted along with Hull House alumnae would prove to be one of startling influence. In 1912, President William Howard Taft signed into law the creation of a federal Children's Bureau. Florence Kelley pushed for labor reforms that were adopted in part by Illinois lawmakers. (Her opposition to "sweated labor" mirrored that of her great aunt, who eschewed the use of cotton and sugar produced by slave labor.) Grace Abbott expanded the Children's Bureau agenda beyond research into childhood problems, into advocacy for the federal funding of family interventions on a grand scale. Alice Hamilton became a public health leader, having been the first to identify a broken sewage pipe leaking into a water main as the cause of a typhoid fever outbreak in Chicago, concentrated around Hull House.

Jane Addams set her sights internationally, devoting the later years of her life to the new Wilsonian goal of world peace. Her Hull House reputation earned her global renown in the 1920s and early 1930s. Just four years before her death in 1935, she was awarded the Nobel Peace Prize. What Addams most deplored about war was its "total prevention of the mutual understanding of peoples," according to James Linn, a biographer. "She saw that in peace such mutual understanding was possible, that in war it was impossible; and she was certain that without that mutual understanding there could be no real progress."[30] In other words, she saw her work at Hull House as naturally related to a quest for peace, and indeed the two missions were linked when she was feted in Oslo. A peaceful world would not drive refugees and immigrants toward the freedom of the United States, where they might find themselves in neighborhoods like Chicago's Near West Side.

The reform efforts of Hull House alumnae represent a dramatic change from the goals of the original settlement house founders. Leaders in social services were now looking to government as a means to remedy social ills. "To midwestern reformers government was an engine of progress they were eager to harness to their projects," as the social historian Michael Katz puts it.[31] Forces were set in motion that drew private, civil society groups into an embrace with government—an embrace tightened by funding—which over time pulled them away from the broad promotion of social norms. Instead, they would aim to ameliorate the specific problems of individual households, and at the same time advocate Progressive policy reforms to correct what they viewed as a dysfunctional economic system. It was a pivot from the formative to the reformative, and to an increasingly "wholesale" approach to social work, more and more tied to government action.

Indeed, it is not a stretch to say that Jane Addams, among the most influential figures in the country, turned away from the promotion of bourgeois norms and toward what Joel Schwartz has incisively called "social rather than individual virtues." Heir to a family fortune, Addams became a critic of "moral reform," deriding those who insisted on personal virtues and behavioral norms as "incorrigibly bourgeois." She disparaged the "middle-class moralist" who maintained that "the specialized virtues of thrift, industry and sobriety" could ensure upward mobility.[32] "The benevolent individual of fifty years ago honestly believed that industry and self-denial in youth would result in comfortable possessions for old age," she wrote in *Democracy and Social Ethics* (1903). In the era of big-city political bosses, she had come to believe, on the contrary, that "the path which leads to riches and success, to civic prominence and honor, is the path of political corruption." Or as latter-day critics would put it, "the system" was rigged. "To attain individual morality in an age demanding social morality, to pride one's self on the results of personal effort when the time demands social adjustment, is utterly to fail to apprehend the situation," Addams wrote.[33]

In fact, she and her settlement peers *acted* on the idea that individual adjustment was a constructive response to poverty and immigrant status, but rhetorically they turned decisively away from that emphasis. Thus they helped initiate a long, slow decline in the promotion of bourgeois norms by elites, roughly during the years from 1880 to 1930.

This change involved two parallel developments, seemingly opposite but converging at the same point. Private charitable efforts in behalf of the poor were shifting focus away from helping them meet the demands of American society, toward changing that society through political reform. At the same time, the principle of spreading the norms of Americanization and cultural assimilation to communities and groups in difficult straits was giving way to assessing the particular needs of individual households. If a family was judged to need financial assistance, it would also receive new forms of therapy under the name of social work. Both these changes led away from civil society and toward government programs. Both came at the expense of bourgeois norms.

The change was attended by an intense and fascinating debate within the ranks of those seeking the right mix of policies and actions to ameliorate poverty. Even today, long after the heyday of the original settlement house movement, the need for civil society institutions that teach and uphold social norms is still recognized. Charles Murray wrote of a time in the not-too-distant past when a common civic culture united all Americans, rich and poor, in a shared understanding of essential virtues:

> As recently as half a century ago, Americans of all classes showed only minor differences on the Founding virtues. When Americans resisted the idea of being thought part of an upper class or lower class, they were responding to a reality: there really was such as thing as a civic culture that embraced all of them.[34]

Murray was mourning the absence of what the young Jane Addams had worked so passionately to build—but which, ironically, the older Jane Addams and her protégés helped to undermine.

# 3

# MARY RICHMOND: FROM "SCIENTIFIC CHARITY" TO SOCIAL WORK

W hile the private efforts by Charles Loring Brace and Jane Addams typified social service in the mid to late nineteenth century, America did not entirely lack government-funded "safety net" institutions, though it was not yet a wealthy country. Local governments maintained "undifferentiated almshouses" for the elderly poor, the disabled, orphans, and even the mentally ill. There was also "outdoor relief," provided outside the almshouses, though some philanthropists believed deeply that private charity was preferable to such provisions.[1]

Josephine Shaw Lowell, who came from a prominent Boston family, famously expressed this perspective in her influential 1884 book, *Public Relief and Private Charity*. Noninstitutional poor relief, wrote Lowell, allowed the "idle, improvident, and even vicious man...the right to live upon the proceeds of the labor of his industrious and virtuous fellow citizen."[2] Lowell and other philanthropists of her day thought it essential to consider what incentives were being created, as Robert Bremner notes:

> They wished to improve the poorhouses but not to such an extent that people would cease dreading to be sent to them. They wanted to

help the unemployed and the deserving poor, but not to be so kind about it that those groups would be tempted into permanent dependency. They yearned to feed the hungry and warm the cold—but they suspected that many persons who seemed to be famishing and freezing were actually imposters. They desired to do what was necessary to relieve suffering in an efficient, economical and businesslike manner, and they wanted to do it by means of voluntary contributions and services rather than through tax-supported benevolence.[3]

The concern to provide help without perpetuating poverty gave rise to the movement called "scientific charity," and with it a network of "charity organization societies" established in major cities to evaluate individual cases of poverty and track the recipients of aid. It was a movement rooted in the "friendly visiting" tradition that began with Robert Hartley in New York: visits to the homes of poor families, offering advice and a good example to inspire self-sufficiency. The new version of friendly visiting was different, however. Rather than focus on universally helpful norms, the visitors from charity organization societies (COS) began with the premise that some particular weakness of character or mind or body was responsible for an individual's poverty. The goal then was to discover that weakness and bring about a correction.[4] Charity organization societies maintained extensive files on individual families, a "central alphabetical register of the poor." One of its purposes was to guard against fraud and the possibility that someone might be collecting relief from multiple different societies. The COS promoted industriousness by requiring work, perhaps in a "wood yard or a place to break stone."[5]

Over time, however, the COS movement began to embrace much of the attitude of the Progressive reformers emerging from settlement houses. It promoted child-care centers for working mothers, and considered the idea of "mothers' pensions" to allow widowed or abandoned mothers to stay home to raise their children. The COS also advocated economic and labor reforms, calling for higher wages and better working conditions, supporting labor unions, and organizing women.[6]

Support for these reforms did not inevitably precipitate a decline in the dissemination of social norms. The COS's friendly visiting did not disappear, but it evolved, and that evolution brought a new challenge: Should the focus remain on improving the habits and character of the poor, even as laws were passed to create an economic safety net—that is, a welfare state?

A key figure who addressed this question was Mary Ellen Richmond, a contemporary and admirer of Jane Addams, but different in crucial ways. Born in 1869 in Baltimore, Richmond did not learn about the poor by visiting them; she was raised poor herself. She brought her own experience of being an unmarried working-class girl to the debate over whether norms mattered and how they should be promoted. A defender of Victorian norms, as her biographer Elizabeth Agnew characterized her, Richmond would fight a losing battle to maintain them as an element in the emerging field of social work—which she herself helped found.

Her mother came from a once-affluent family of Boston merchants who fell on hard times when Mary's grandfather went west for the 1849 Gold Rush and then died of typhoid fever in California. The marriage of Mary's mother, perhaps driven by economic pressures, was an unlikely match between a Protestant with "middle-class intellectual and cultural tastes" and a Catholic carriage maker who would become a "heavy drinker."[7] After her mother died of tuberculosis, Mary's father deserted the family and she was raised by her grandmother, Mehitable Harris, who supported herself by operating a boarding house on the fringe of Baltimore Harbor, where increasing legions of German and Irish immigrants worked on the docks and lived in rented rooms.

Harris was unusual for her time: an advocate of "woman's rights" and "voluntary motherhood" (birth control through sexual abstinence, even in marriage), and a "spiritualist," convinced that communication with the dead was possible. Along with séances, she hosted freewheeling conversations in the boarding house parlor, which fed Mary's intellect and acquainted her with major social issues of the time, including "woman's rights, rights for free blacks, labor reform, socialism, temperance, dress reform and vegetarianism."[8] Harris was critical of the rote learning that was typical in public schools, and she kept her granddaughter out of school until age eleven, a decision which didn't appear to impede the girl's intellectual development.

A friend of Harris's provided a steady stream of books—including works of Dickens, Walter Scott, and George Eliot—on the condition that Mary write a summary of each. If Richmond's own situation were not enough to prompt her to think about poverty, the literature she read would do so. She later wrote of her sorrow in reading the "pathetic story of little Dombey," and of David Copperfield's "miserable employment in the warehouse of Murdstone and Grimby," a story she came to see as "not half so miserable as the reality."[9] In the introduction to her book *Friendly Visiting Among the Poor* (1899), she praised the "march of the plain and common people into the foreground of English fiction." But she went on to criticize Dickens for "exaggeration and unreality" in his depiction of poverty and for sentimentalism about the motives of laborers and artisans. Uplifting the poor was a complex undertaking, she realized.

When Mary Richmond eventually entered public school at Baltimore's Eastern Female High School, she prospered academically despite being less well-off than other students. "She experienced heartening confirmation of the importance of personal character over class circumstances," writes Agnew. "It was a lesson that she carried with her in her life and work."[10]

Notwithstanding her academic success, Richmond nonetheless came to the profession of social service out of her own economic need—and quite indirectly. After her high school graduation, she needed a job to help support her grandmother. Through a maternal aunt, she obtained a clerical position at a publishing house connected with the Unitarian Church in New York. There she developed symptoms of tuberculosis, the disease that had killed her mother. (It was thought to be inheritable at the time, so Mary had been living under a cloud.) She recovered, but a wave of malaria in the city prompted her to return to Baltimore.

Through her tenuous links to the upper-middle-class world of her late mother's family and her affluent friends from high school, Richmond was eventually drawn into a career that would prove influential—and in some ways that she neither anticipated nor entirely welcomed. But first she spent seven years in her twenties in bookkeeper positions, one at a stationery store, where she was unjustly accused of theft and lost the job (about which she remained bitter the rest of her life). A chance meeting with old high school friends who shared her literary passions brought her into a salon, and then a social circle that included civic-minded philanthropists who, in turn, introduced her to the Baltimore Charity Organization Society.

She began in a clerical role, in 1888, keeping track of those voluminous files on individual poor households requesting "alms."[11] In a Horatio

Alger–type story, however, the young woman in the secretarial role was spotted and mentored by the chairman of the organization's board. Like all COS board members, John M. Glenn was among the social and economic elite of the booming city of Baltimore, and he backed Richmond as executive secretary of the organization over a Johns Hopkins graduate who was part of the emergent academic discipline of social science.[12] Glenn's choice launched Richmond into a career of national influence.

She had seen that individual life decisions—including her own—truly affect one's fortunes. To be sure, she agreed with Addams and her acolytes that Progressive policy reforms were warranted, and she called for efforts to "prevent preventable disease, to lighten the burden of unavoidable misfortune, [and] to secure better living conditions, better social opportunities, [and] a larger outlook for the poor."[13] But her professional focus remained on "friendly visiting," an activity that developed under her leadership into the profession now called social work.

In putting a premium on direct interaction with the poor, Richmond very much reflected the worldview of an influential contemporary, Robert Hunter of New York, a onetime University Settlement resident who in 1904 published the first great statistical overview of the American poor. In this book, simply titled *Poverty*, he stressed a distinction between the poor and so-called "paupers." The poor were those who strove daily but were cruelly buffeted by economic ups and downs. For them, Hunter cared deeply:

> There are great districts of people who are up before dawn, who wash, dress and eat breakfast, kiss wives and children, and hurry away to work or to seek work. The world rests upon their shoulders; it moves by their muscle.... But the world is so organized that they gain enough to live upon only when they work; should they cease, they are in destitution and want.[14]

Paupers were different, as their disorganized lives and unhealthy habits kept them poor in good times and bad:

> There are in all large cities in America and abroad, streets and courts and alleys where a class of people live who have lost all self-respect and ambition, who rarely, if ever, work, who are aimless and drifting,

who like drink, who have no thought for their children, and who live more or less contentedly on rubbish and alms.

These were the people who became dependent on alms—who "live miserably, but they do not care."[15]

The same distinction guided Richmond in her first significant professional position. She made it her priority to increase the number of friendly visitors in Baltimore, both to root out "imposture" and to encourage among the poor "their sense of independence, self-reliance, ability to stand on their own feet, and the desire to pay their own bills, in so far as they are able to."[16] She cited with approval the motto of the British reformer Octavia Hill: "Not alms but a friend."[17]

Richmond well understood that the involvement of middle-class people in the lives of the poor was itself a signal of norms. In *Friendly Visiting Among the Poor*, she recommended specific ways to go about "restoring a tone of sturdy self-reliance and independence" among the poor.[18] Visitors could exercise a formative influence, for example, by organizing a "library circle" with a group of neighborhood children, meeting regularly to discuss books with them, play games, and get "well acquainted."[19] Richmond named a striking range of civil society institutions that could also be helpful in imparting norms, such as fresh-air societies and Sunday schools.[20]

Like Brace, she was comfortable with removing children from dysfunctional households: "It sometimes becomes the visitor's painful duty to protect children from cruelty, criminal neglect, or immorality by legal removal from their parents' control."[21] She encouraged a detailed investigation of individual poor households, which led to the finding that 6 percent of householders were "intemperate" and 8 percent were "shiftless," while 53 percent simply lacked "adequate work and wages."[22] Although she emphasized "the so-called industrial virtues of thrift, sobriety, and hard work," as Agnew writes, Richmond acknowledged that "structural and environmental conditions" could cause poverty.[23] She advocated a compulsory education law in Maryland to help reduce poverty in future generations.

After becoming the head of the larger Philadelphia Charity Organization Society in 1900, Richmond continued to insist on the importance of friendly visiting, both as a means of encouraging the development of good character and as a way of building a personal relationship between giver and recipient, which she considered crucial. In order to provide effective assistance to a household, it was necessary to *know* that household.

This view is central to her magnum opus, *Social Diagnosis* (1917), which in many ways served as the founding document of professional social work. Explaining her choice of the term "social diagnosis," she wrote: "The effort to get the essential facts bearing upon a man's social difficulties has commonly been called 'an investigation,' but the term here adopted as a substitute—social diagnosis—has the advantage that from the first step it fixes the mind of the case worker upon the end in view."[24] By speaking of "social diagnosis," Richmond was dressing up her ideas in the sort of quasi-medical language that had become fashionable. She was not referring to psychiatry, however, for she believed that the right norms remained the appropriate prescription for achieving the desired result.

She taught caseworkers how to collect and evaluate "social evidence" as the basis for a "diagnosis" of the situation. "Social evidence," she explained, included "any and all facts as to personal or family history which, taken together, indicate the nature of a given client's social difficulties and the means to their solution."[25] These facts were to be gathered both in direct conversations with the family and through the "concentric circles" of its relationships in the neighborhood and beyond. Relatives and neighbors, schools and employers, medical personnel, social agencies and fraternal orders—all these could supply information to illuminate how the family might best be helped.[26]

*Social Diagnosis* in part reflects Richmond's ongoing volunteer work as a friendly visitor in the Gramercy Park area of New York after she moved to the city in 1909, and in part the work of research staff at the Russell Sage Foundation in New York, where she held her final and most influential professional position as director of the foundation's Charity Organization Department. That such a position even existed at the time says much about the evolution of American social service. Olivia Sage, widow of the railroad magnate Russell Sage, had been inspired by the philanthropy of Carnegie and Rockefeller to devote a substantial part of her considerable fortune to the study of social conditions and how best to ameliorate them. This effort led to a new debate between antipoverty intellectuals and policy activists, with Richmond herself being swept into a heated public dispute.

The emergent profession of social work was caught up in the broader intellectual crosscurrents of the time as Richmond was writing and speaking in public. Since the turn of the twentieth century, social work had been influenced by the Social Gospel movement, an interpretation of Christianity that called for establishing a Kingdom of God on earth. From this perspective, the main purpose of "friendly visiting" with the poor was to gather evidence supporting the case for structural changes in society, eventually making charity unnecessary. Charles Richmond Henderson of the University of Chicago articulated this idea in 1913:

> Long experience in charity makes us all impatient for the day when charitable relief, with all its humiliations and harrowing uncertainties, will no longer be needed, when a fairer distribution of income, a complete system of social hygiene, education and insurance, will reduce dependence to a vanishing point, and the hope of promoting that purpose is the chief inspiration of contemporary charity. We know these tragic case records and the statistics that are gathered from them must quicken the public conscience and lead to nobler methods.[27]

Alongside the Social Gospel with its emphasis on changing society, another current of thought focused intensely on the individual, through the influence of Sigmund Freud. His widely acclaimed "Introductory Lectures on Psycho-Analysis," delivered between 1915 and 1917, popularized his theories on personality. "Psychiatric social work" started to become the organizing principle of the new profession, promising a deeper understanding of "the client's situation and condition," and along with it "the solution to the most vexing forms of personal difficulty," as Andrew Polsky puts it.[28]

The embrace of psychiatry reflects the aspiration of the self-styled social work profession to cast itself in the mold of medicine—as a discipline informed by scientific principles. This extra layer of academic respectability was what social work needed at the time, when questions were being raised as to whether it was a bona fide profession at all. Abraham Flexner, a prominent educator and public intellectual, gave a devastating address in 1915 to the National Conference of Charities and Correction in Baltimore, posing a deeply skeptical question in its title: "Is Social Work a Profession?" Flexner, renowned for proposing reforms to medical education that were adopted by the Harvard Medical School, observed that "to make a profession in the genuine sense, something more than a mere claim or an academic degree is needed. There are certain objective standards that can be formulated."[29] Insofar as social work lacked the rigor of law or medicine, he implied, it was not a profession.

Flexner put social work on the defensive, along with Richmond and others who had faith in Victorian virtues. But Richmond had also been developing a definite set of techniques for the profession, and she became social work's champion. With *Social Diagnosis*, she provided a guide for the growing number of university programs in social work and philanthropy, while trying valiantly to preserve the "friendly visiting" commitment to shaping character—even as policy reform and Freudianism swirled around her. "Although she presumed the necessity of professional training," writes Agnew, "she continued to promote the work of trained volunteers, as well as of paid professionals." She also strove to preserve the private, self-governing character of local charity organizations, and to uphold the importance of privately administered relief for the needy.[30]

In a narrow way, Richmond was successful with *Social Diagnosis*. As a book of technique, it instructed social workers and friendly visitors in how to interview and understand the household they set out to help. It also brought Richmond even wider recognition than her work for Russell Sage already had. But it was not powerful enough to win the debate over her profession's future. Flexner had "hastened the turn to technique," remarks Agnew, "and Richmond's response to his report inadvertently contributed to this process."[31]

When Richmond gave a public address in 1917 titled "The Social Worker's Task," in answer to Flexner's challenge, she portrayed this task as quite different from that of the traditional friendly visitor who brought a message of middle-class norms. The social worker, she said, would provide a "gateway to social treatment" thanks to specific abilities: "first, skill in discovering the social relationships by which a given personality had been shaped; second, ability to get at the central core of the difficulty in these relationships; and third, power to utilize the direct action of mind upon mind in their adjustment."[32] This, of course, is the language of therapy, not social norms, and it represented a crucial turning point. The new focus on "mental factors" was quite different from the earlier emphasis on "character reform," and the language of "mind upon mind" sounded much like the mental hygiene movement that was becoming popular at the time, as Agnew points out. "Richmond's emphasis on personality and its adjustment rather than on character and moral reform reflected the emerging influence of scientific management and the consumer culture."[33]

Mary Richmond herself, however, never accepted a fully psychoanalytic view of the self. Nor did she become a convert to government-provided financial relief, though she acknowledged the role of effective government institutions in bettering the lives of the poor. In *Friendly Visiting Among the Poor*, she stated a conviction that individual effort with poor households must be complemented by policies to improve social conditions generally:

> The problems of poverty must be attacked from both sides,... and though I shall dwell particularly upon individual service in these pages, we should remember that, unless this service is supplemented by the work of good citizens, who shall strive to make our cities healthier and freer from temptation, our school system more thorough and practical, and our public charities more effective, unless this public work also is pushed forward, our individual work in the homes of the poor will be largely in vain.[34]

She later made the point more concisely in *Social Diagnosis*: "Mass betterment and individual betterment are interdependent."[35]

In Richmond's view, charity societies with their home visitors and settlement workers each tended to exaggerate certain factors in poverty— respectively, those that are internal and those that are external to poor individuals themselves.[36] Friendly visitors were inclined to overstate the role of personal failings as the cause of poverty or other problems of poor households, she wrote: "We are likely to over-emphasize the moral and mental lacks shown in bad personal habits, such as drunkenness and licentiousness, in thriftlessness, laziness, or inefficiency; and some of us are even rash enough to attribute all the ills of the poor to drink or laziness." But others placed too much weight on external factors as causes of poverty and distress: "Settlement workers are likely to say that the sufferings of the poor are due to conditions over which the poor have no control," such as "bad industrial conditions and defective legislation." Richmond stressed that "personal and social causes of poverty" are interconnected and "form a tangle that no hasty impatient jerking can unravel."[37]

Therefore it was essential to steer between the extremes of overemphasis on either individual failings or social conditions, and to balance the different approaches to alleviating poverty.

> Friendly visitors and all who are trying to improve conditions in poor homes should welcome the experience of those who are studying trade conditions and other more general aspects of questions affecting the welfare of the poor. But they should not permit themselves to be swept away by enthusiastic advocates of social reform from that safe middle ground which recognizes that character is at the very centre of this complicated problem; character in the rich, who owe the poor justice as well as mercy, and character in the poor, who are masters of their fate to a greater degree than they will recognize or than we will recognize for them. To ignore the importance of character and of the discipline that makes character is a common fault of modern philanthropy.[38]

Richmond was resolute in her belief that the question of character and values should never be neglected, even as efforts were made to improve social conditions. Thus it was intellectually consistent for her to oppose both the major currents influencing the nature of social work in her time. Having been formed by a Victorian moral culture, she resisted the trend to bring Freudian psychoanalysis, with its focus on the subconscious, into friendly visiting. And while she accepted the "wholesale reform" movement for laws concerning wages and working hours, occupational safety, and unemployment compensation, she opposed the growth of the welfare state and the campaign to establish universal forms of government benefits for the poor. Notably, she staged an unsuccessful rearguard action against the growing movement for "mothers' pensions," or state aid for single parents, which had begun as a provision exclusively for widows.

She believed that aid should not be based on need alone, but should be granted through a "retail" approach in which "material relief can be transmuted into human values." By "human values," Richmond meant "cultural and educational enrichment and the strengthening of family and civic ties—values that financial relief alone would not necessarily foster," as Agnew writes.[39]

Along with a colleague at the Russell Sage Foundation, Richmond collected case histories of 985 single mothers who were assisted by charity organization societies, and cited 54 cases in which "agents removed children from widowed mothers owing to the mothers' 'character,'" and the same number in which "children were placed in institutions owing to 'doubtful home influences,'" including "suspicion of their laziness, extravagance, unreliability, bad temper, and neglect or poor control of their children."[40] She was not blind to the problems posed by larger economic conditions, including "insufficient food, clothing, and shelter," and she acknowledged that family breakdown could sometimes be a result of poverty. But she favored private assistance over public aid—even, apparently, if it meant that children might be institutionalized.[41]

For Mary Richmond, the Victorian virtues—including a religious calling to precisely the work she was helping to professionalize—were timeless. But despite her efforts to secure their place in social work, her vision of civil society organizations continuing to sponsor visitors who modeled bourgeois norms for the troubled and disorganized poor would gradually fade away. When she died in 1927—a single woman with a world of close professional friends—her views were not yet washed away in a tide of public policy action, but the trend had already started at the state level. Illinois passed the first statewide mothers' pension law in 1911. The New York State Commission on Relief for Widowed Mothers pushed through pensions in 1915. At the federal level, a welfare program for single mothers, Aid to Dependent Children, was part of the Franklin Roosevelt administration's 1935 Social Security Act. Crucially, amendments to that act passed in 1962 would direct a torrent of government grants to what were once financially independent social service organizations, such as the Juvenile Aid Society (later part of the Jewish Family and Children's Service of Philadelphia).

Over time, federal initiatives supplanted Richmond's ideal of the friendly visitor offering advice and modeling norms. The social worker became both gatekeeper and therapist—someone who connected those receiving help with the range of financial assistance programs available, and who focused on individual personalities rather than universal virtues. In a brilliant analysis, the sociologist Andrew Polsky describes the result as "the rise of the therapeutic state," with its emphasis on "personality reconstruction or behavioral modification."[42] In Polsky's view, Freudian "normalizing" techniques have been employed to push the poor and working-class away from collective political action.

Polsky, it must be noted, has no more fondness for neo-Victorian values than for "personality reconstruction." Nevertheless, he keenly observes how the advocates of a *therapeutic* social service state became ascendant. "Perhaps the most important gain recorded by therapeutic activists was their success in enlisting the support of the federal government," he writes.[43] Activists capitalized on the economic distress of the Great Depression, "which pointed up the inadequacies of previous forms of social provision for the needy," in order to marry federal support for social services to "social insurance" programs such as the old-age pensions introduced in the Social Security Act. Those activists "insinuated themselves into key policymaking positions during the New Deal to bring federal resources into the human services."[44]

By the late 1930s, the Progressive reform movement had carried the day, as old-age pensions, public housing, and mothers' pensions became law. The role of government would expand further in the 1960s, when social and political circumstances combined to stream large amounts of federal dollars through the Department of Health, Education, and Welfare—later the Department of Health and Human Services, and its Administration for Children and Families. This expansion not only replaced the private, civil society action preferred by Mary Richmond, but swallowed up large sections of civil society itself, as independent agencies providing social services evolved into government contractors. It's what Steven Rathgeb Smith and Michael Lipsky have called "the welfare state in the age of contracting."[45]

This was all far from an overnight process, but the trend proved to be inexorable. Though the triumph of Progressivism is now well known, controversy has flared, off and on, over how assistance is best provided—revisiting Josephine Shaw Lowell's and Mary Richmond's concerns about providing assistance on the basis of need alone. The question of whether public assistance or even health insurance should be contingent on work has periodically captured public attention and inspired debate.

A lower-profile but equally important controversy was playing out simultaneously. On the one side were those who believed that preparing the poor for success could best be done by promoting middle-class social norms through neighborhood action (the early settlement houses) and individual social work (friendly visiting). On the other, which turned out to be the winning side, were those who favored individual therapy keyed to particular problems, such as child abuse and neglect, or failures in marriage and parental responsibility, or runaway and homeless youth—which became specific targets of government action.[46] Addressing these problems would be the province of specialized professionals, often with graduate degrees in social work. My father's mentor, Mrs. Sternberger, called herself a social worker, but today she would be considered professionally unqualified.

As Andrew Polsky writes, "social personnel" have pushed for "an expansion in the scope of public tutelage, to seek more resources and a greater public investment in training skilled caseworkers and to agitate for a major role for themselves whenever some new manifestation of marginality has come to our notice."[47] In other words, they have aimed to enlarge the scope of government intervention and to make themselves more important.

Consider the stated goals of a contemporary social worker employed by the Latino Family Services center in Detroit: "We work toward meeting the advocacy and mental health needs of the broad Latino community that is located here."[48] Although the center offers classes in English as a Second Language (a residue of the settlement influence), its programs are largely focused on *problems*, offering "outpatient substance abuse treatment, HIV/AIDS counseling, testing and outreach, developmental disabilities case management," and the like.[49]

The overall objective was no longer to spread norms—a goal that Polsky finds morally objectionable—but to "remold clients' volitions, aspirations, and sense of personal identity," as he summarizes it. He notes pointedly, "Little of this could be accomplished by philanthropy alone, to be sure, as its resources were insufficient. So proponents of the new casework approach urged an alliance with the state, and pronounced themselves ready to serve the new public service agencies they hoped to create."[50]

The advocates of social reform and the proponents of individual therapy both aimed to touch as many individuals as possible, whether as "beneficiaries" or as "clients." For both, it was not enough to promote social norms and trust that they would spread by example. For both, the pathway to a wide reach pointed in the same direction: away from civil society and toward government.

# 4

# GRACE ABBOTT FROM NEBRASKA: SERVICES RATHER THAN NORMS

The woman who did more than anyone else to shape the federal direction and funding of the modern social service state was not an obvious candidate for someone who would dramatically expand the U.S. federal government. A daughter of small-town Nebraska, born in 1878 in Grand Island, Grace Abbott began her professional life teaching school in Broken Bow, an even smaller Nebraska town. Twenty years later, after a residency at Hull House, she was in Washington, D.C., pursuing a new career—and, moreover, a new kind of career. As head of the federal Children's Bureau, established in 1912 by President William Howard Taft, she changed American government in ways that would touch the lives of children and their families across the country. Abbott helped establish new types of government programs, such as federal grants to the states for approved purposes (later called "categorical" programs), and assistance payments for individuals that would become known as entitlements.

Grace Abbott mapped a new route to social change through the public sector together with her older sister, Edith, who profoundly shaped the emerging field of professional social work and public administration of social services from her position at the University of Chicago. The sisters combined academic studies focused on particular social ills (such as child labor, or death in childbirth) with powerful federal initiatives designed to cure them. It is a combination that later became commonplace, but was something quite new in the Abbotts' day. In fairly short order, the idea that social problems could be quantified and analyzed, and that Washington should take the lead in fixing them with a specific program, became ingrained in the American psyche. The "Abbott sisters from Nebraska," as Grace and Edith were commonly known, should get a good deal of credit for the change—whether for better or worse.

The sisters grew up in a relatively genteel household in Grand Island—not unlike Jane Addams's family in rural Illinois—though Grace and Edith's parents were in many ways extraordinary. Their father, Othman Abbott, by his own account was a direct descendant of James Chilton, a signatory of the Mayflower Compact.[1] His family had strong political views. "Father was an out-and-out anti-slavery man," wrote Othman in his colorfully detailed memoir, *Recollections of a Pioneer Lawyer*. "It was part of his religion, so to speak, that slavery was a national sin, a relic of barbarism."[2] (Notably, opposition to slavery was common to the Brace, Addams, and Abbott families.) After serving in the Civil War, Othman Abbott moved by stagecoach from DeKalb, Illinois, to Nebraska, settling in Grand Island, then a town with just a few buildings and not even a rail connection; he stopped there because Indian hostilities made it unsafe to venture farther west. The town grew to nearly ten thousand inhabitants thanks to the German immigrants who farmed the land around it, and Abbott became a prominent small-town lawyer and banker. He helped organize the Nebraska state government, serving in two constitutional conventions, and was the state's first elected lieutenant governor.

His wife, Elizabeth, was born in a log house, also in Dekalb, where prairie fires were commonly visible from the front porch. She was from a Quaker family with strongly abolitionist views like those of her husband, who recalled:

> I did not know until after our marriage that Mrs. Abbott's mother with her Aunty Lydia and her Uncle Allen had really worked for the Underground Railroad in our part of Illinois. My wife had been cautioned as a child never to tell of things.... She remembers as they were

taking her mother's horses out one day and seemed to be giving them away to relieve a strange team, she went under what she thought was a strange hay wagon to pick up a bail and suddenly in the crack she saw two black brows and four bright eyes looking down.[3]

For the small-town Midwest, where ice cream socials and church suppers were the normal entertainment, the Abbotts were cosmopolitan — subscribing to *Harper's Weekly* and the *North American Review*.[4] Although the family was not religious and Othman Abbott worked at his law office on Sundays, he and "Lizzie" sent their daughters to an Episcopal boarding school in Omaha, and exposed them to a wide range of literature, from Dickens to Darwin to Virgil. (Othman recalled that he treasured a copy of *David Copperfield* while serving in the Union Army.) Lizzie considered herself a suffragist, and six-year-old Edith once had to give up her bed for Susan B. Anthony, who stayed with the Abbotts when she gave a speech in Grand Island in 1882.[5] Mr. Abbott would invite his daughters to the courthouse to see the law in action.

Supporters of Abraham Lincoln, the Abbotts were staunch Republicans and not given to Populist ideas about how to help the small farmers who were mainstays of Othman's legal practice. In 1896, Mr. Abbott campaigned throughout Nebraska in opposition to the Democratic presidential candidate and Nebraska native son, William Jennings Bryan, and decried Bryan's proposal to abandon the gold standard (in order to relieve farmers of burdensome debt) as an attack on "sound money." Bryan, he made clear to his daughters, was a "windbag" and a "demagogue." The girls remembered their father denouncing "men who do not want to work themselves and do not want anyone else to work," and "men who haven't the courage to take a dose of hard times and who think someone has always got to make them comfortable or keep them out of debt."[6] Grace would later become an impassioned public orator herself, but espousing ideas not remotely similar to those of her father.

Upon moving to Broken Bow, population around one thousand, twenty-year-old Grace would not have found a public library, only a reading room maintained by the Women's Christian Temperance Union. She taught seven classes daily, from geometry to German, which then was commonly spoken by many of the area's immigrant farmers. As a schoolteacher, she was expected "to provide a decorous model of behavior, avoid frivolous activities such as dancing, take an active interest in the affairs of the town but not introduce alien influences, maintain strict discipline in the classrooms, work uncomplainingly for long hours, put up with less than comfortable living arrangements, and attend church regularly," writes her biographer, Lela Costin.[7] Abbott might have remained the schoolteacher of Broken Bow had not a wave of typhoid fever swept through town, making her ill. Upon recovering, she taught in Grand Island's high school, where she also directed school plays and coached girls' basketball. She was teaching school in Nebraska until 1907, when she was twenty-nine.

Chicago was a magnet for the small-town Abbott girls. Lizzie had brought her daughters to the city for the World's Fair in 1893, and the boomtown clearly left an impression on them. Ten years later, Edith was drawn to graduate education at the young University of Chicago, which was "a champion of new ideas and new disciplines—particularly sociology, social work, anthropology and psychology."[8] She earned a doctorate in economics, and later founded a pioneering graduate program, the School of Social Service Administration, at the university. Meanwhile, Grace had followed her to Chicago and earned a political science degree, then set out to put her education into administrative action.

When Grace became a resident of Hull House in 1907—as did Edith soon afterward—it had changed markedly since the late 1880s. Jane Addams and the group surrounding her had been strongly drawn to reform, and it was this Hull House movement in which Grace Abbott became first a foot soldier and then a leader. Her first executive role was as the director of the Immigrants' Protective League, a new type of organization combining assistance for immigrants with what would later be called "advocacy."

Abbott came to be critical of those she deemed too insistent on the cultural assimilation of new immigrants:

> Many Americans are not satisfied with the teaching of English alone. They want instructions in what they call the fundamental American principles.... I have usually found they feel it would be a good thing to put immediately into the immigrant's hands the story of Lincoln and Washington, and that patriotic instruction should be the basis of all of their future work. [But] the fundamental Americanisms, I am

convinced, cannot be taught by the method of direct assault, so to speak, and we should not be discouraged at failures when it is used.

She argued that if religious toleration is thought of as "the first of those characteristics which we regard as distinctly American," then her own Puritan ancestors had not been quick to "Americanize." Likewise, one should not expect the Italian immigrant to become Americanized "in a course of ten lessons in the fundamentals." Nor should there be great concern about matters of "speech, dress, and house-keeping" among new arrivals, for "Americanization in these things will come rapidly enough."[9]

For Abbott, there were matters of more immediate importance to new immigrants than instruction on social norms and American political principles. Her Immigrants' Protective League served as a port in a storm for newcomers, and a helping hand for people in difficulty. Notably, this would be the only time in Grace Abbott's career as a professional advocate for the poor that she had regular personal contact with those in need. For instance, she might provide taxi fare to someone who had run out of money before finding a destination, perhaps having been given a wrong address. She suggested that a federal protection bureau for immigrants could alleviate this kind of problem.[10]

Abbott also dedicated herself to guarding immigrants against prospective employers who might take advantage of them, such as by promising work at relatively high wages if they moved to a remote area, but not delivering on the promise. In her view, America had an obligation to prove itself worthy of immigrants' hopes, and this would in turn help make them good citizens:

> What we must do, if the immigrant is to become a desirable citizen, is to preserve his simple honesty and thrift, and his faith in America and American institutions. As the first step in this process, he needs to know almost immediately on his arrival the practices of employment agents and the remedies that are open to him in cases of abuse; the requirement for licenses in certain trades; something of our labor laws; something of our sanitary regulations; how he may protect himself against violations by his neighbors of the health code; and how he may send money home to his wife and mother.

The public schools should be helping in this process by providing information to immigrants in their own language, with "illustrated lectures,"
she suggested.[11]

In effect, Abbott took for granted that immigrants possessed the
character and capacity to make good decisions that could lead to upward
mobility. She focused her concern instead on assistance. What's more,
Abbott saw the work of her philanthropically supported Immigrants'
Protective League as but a way station toward government-supported
provision—which would inevitably emphasize service rather than the
promotion of social norms. Both Abbott sisters, as Costin writes, regarded immigrants as "oppressed and in need of protective services, not
because immigrants were personally inadequate and helpless individuals
but because they came into an inferior social, economic and political status upon their arrival in this country." And the Abbotts "seldom doubted
that they knew the correct solution to many of the immigrants' problems,
particularly those requiring a familiarity with governmental organizations
and a capacity for utilizing official agencies."[12]

Grace Abbott's concerns about immigrants' needs were not entirely
misplaced, and public action and institutions such as the schools might
have been appropriate to the situations she addressed. (After all, it was
the Philadelphia public schools that fostered my father's love of classical
music and the passion for science that led to a career in engineering, while
the Juvenile Aid Society helped ensure a safe and clean foster home.) But
in proposing a hierarchy of importance to immigrants in their adjustment
to American life, and making government the vehicle for the services
she prioritized, Abbott was effectively saying that some services but not
others deserved taxpayer support. This is the fundamental complication
resulting from the entrance of government into realms where civil society
once dominated: that which government funds becomes important at the
expense of what it does not. Social norms of the sort that Brace and the
Juvenile Aid Society emphasized would now be de-emphasized, in favor
of social services designed to cure ills rather than prevent them.

The services that Abbott promoted were not objectionable in themselves, but she emphasized them at the expense of the formative work in
which earlier settlement house volunteers engaged. She simply took for
granted such virtues as thrift, sobriety, and responsibility in family life.
And like the Progressives in general, she reflexively called in government

as her partner. "Public service has certain opportunities greater than those of any private organization," she later wrote, adding, "those of us who believe in the government falling to and doing things ought to be willing to help."[13]

Over the course of her thirty-year professional life, Abbott's approach would triumph, as government displaced and effectively took over much of civil society. By the time she left government, the Social Security Act, signed into law in 1935 by President Franklin Roosevelt, laid the basis for the American welfare state, including not only old-age pensions but much more. It included Aid to Dependent Children—benefits for single mothers, accompanied by counseling and eligibility tests provided by social workers. This was the "mothers' pensions" program, whether for the widowed miner's wife or the deserted urban mother. It was the program opposed by Mary Richmond but strongly favored by Grace Abbott and the "Hull House crowd," who treated financial need as evidence of the market economy's structural failings, rather than calling for steps to prepare the poor to succeed in it. Government was the vehicle to provide "not charity but justice."[14] The federal government would create what became known as a safety net, to offer protection against the fluctuations of the business cycle and the family setbacks that come with death or desertion.[15] The more intangible yet more significant help for the poor—equipping them to meet the challenges and exigencies of life—was lost in the process.

The political forces behind the passage of the Social Security Act were deep and varied. Without doubt, the privation of the Depression had the greatest influence. More generally, private charity appeared inadequate to buffer large segments of the population against the volatility of a modern industrial economy. There were also popular movements clamoring for old-age assistance. Ideas long in gestation were coming to fruition in a time of crisis, after the "seedtime for reform" that typically precedes the passage of social legislation, as the historian Clarke Chambers observes.[16] For instance, the idea of old-age pensions based on individual contributions was proposed in the 1913 book *Social Insurance*,[17] by I. M. Rubinow, a Metropolitan Insurance actuary who would go on to found the American Association for Labor Legislation along with Abraham Epstein. (The latter actually coined the phrase "social security," which he thought more publicly palatable than "social insurance.")[18]

The sections of the Social Security Act dealing with children not only provided for federal monetary support but also for a federally funded legion of social workers, dispatched by the states. It was a sharp turn away from the world of Brace and early Jane Addams and the vision of Mary Richmond—a pivot from organizations focused on promoting middle-class norms in poor neighborhoods, to programs for assessing whether individual households should receive government grants. This was the triumph of Grace Abbott achieved through the Children's Bureau.

From its creation in 1912 during the Taft administration, the Children's Bureau was a new sort of federal agency. It was not meant to deliver or support an ongoing, routine public service, such as collecting customs duties or building the military. Instead, it was created to identify and study problems—and to use its academic and moral authority to summon government to do something about them.

The Children's Bureau grew out of the White House Conference on Children convened in 1909 by Theodore Roosevelt, very much at the behest of the settlement leaders who believed that giving more attention to problems affecting children would lay the foundation for corrective action. Before that time, congressionally mandated commissions—such as the U.S. Immigration Commission (1907) or the President's Homes Commission (1909)—had been formed to examine social problems that might call for government action. The Children's Bureau was different: it was to be a permanent government agency, housed in the Department of Labor, with a strikingly broad mission: "investigate and report upon all matters pertaining to the welfare of children and child life among all classes of our people." These matters were to include "infant mortality, the birth rate, orphanage, juvenile courts, desertion, dangerous occupations, accidents and diseases of children, employment, legislation affecting children in the several States and Territories."[19] Agencies already in existence could have addressed many of these issues; indeed, officials at the U.S. Public Health Service believed their agency should do so. But the Children's Bureau, whose creation was spearheaded by settlement house veterans such as Lillian Wald and Florence Kelley, was meant to create an agenda not for a single agency but for government broadly. Its animating idea was that of an activist federal government calling attention to, and ameliorating, problems associated with the conditions of the poor.

In 1917, Grace Abbott left Chicago to join the Children's Bureau in Washington, taking on a role that was itself novel: overseeing state governments in the matter of child labor. The 1900 census had found two million children and young adults "working in mills, mines, factories, stores, and on city streets across the United States," particularly in the poorer southern states, where teenagers supplemented the income of families who had migrated from the mountains to mill towns. A National Child Labor Committee (backed by settlement leaders) had successfully promoted federal legislation in 1916 to ban the interstate sale of goods produced with the labor of children under the age of fourteen (or sixteen in the case of mines). Abbott's charge was to enforce this law, but the Supreme Court soon struck it down on the grounds that Congress had overstepped its authority to regulate interstate commerce, and Abbott went back to Illinois for a time.

She returned to Washington in 1921 to replace her fellow Hull House alumna Julia Lathrop as director of the Children's Bureau. Abbott was deeply dedicated to her work, arguably a workaholic, living alone near Washington's Rock Creek Park and National Zoo, where she regularly walked. She was a trailblazer, as is so often said of early women professionals—but not just as a feminist. She was speaking for the poor as a professional advocate and agency administrator. Whether through public speaking, appearances at professional social work conferences, or testimony before Congress, she was working to protect and expand the domain of the Children's Bureau.

In addition, she published essays to promote the policies she favored, typically in the *Social Science Review*, the publication begun by her sister, Edith, the dean of the School of Social Service Administration at the University of Chicago. Indeed, Grace's ideas might find their way into print under Edith's name, as the sisters were so close, sharing a vision and a mission which they pursued in complementary ways. As Jeanne Marsh describes the collaboration,

> The Abbott sisters, with their mutual concerns and from their respective platforms, shared resources, ideas and ideals. If, for instance, a student came up with a particularly incisive question, Dean Abbott in Chicago would often make the question known to Chief Abbott in Washington, D.C.—so the Children's Bureau might be able to

support the study and then put the findings to work shaping national policy.[20]

Grace Abbott built and directed the next major initiative of the Children's Bureau: calling upon Congress to levy a tax on the products of child labor. The bureau also mounted an army of child-labor agents to fan out across the country and ensure that states were complying with their own laws limiting child labor. But then the Supreme Court, still not persuaded by Progressive thinking, ruled that the bureau had no such jurisdiction. That Court decision effectively stripped the Children's Bureau of its major ongoing operational role. Abbott then set out on a crusade for federal legislation—even a constitutional amendment, if necessary—to ban child labor.

Her legislative efforts failed, but these setbacks in no way dissuaded Abbott from her belief that improving the health and welfare of children, and of their families, required government involvement as well as funding from Washington. She believed deeply in the view that Mary Richmond had expressed with more reservations in 1899: that poverty had both personal and social causes, and that public initiatives were therefore needed to make individual efforts in poor households effective. Abbott would live to see her emphasis on legislative action embodied in the Social Security Act of 1935, but en route there were false starts and revealing debates, which made clear that some in positions of authority understood the magnitude of the change and did not welcome it.

Some of those twists and turns surrounded the Sheppard-Towner Maternity and Infancy Protection Act, which was passed in 1921, just as Abbott was taking the helm at the Children's Bureau. Prompted by reports of alarming levels of maternal death in childbirth and of infant mortality (an example of social science studies leading to government action), the act was, in effect, a declaration that "the people of the United States through their federal government, share with the states and localities the responsibility for helping to provide community services that children need for a good start in life."[21] The federal government would review state plans in the service of that broad mission, and award matching grants if both the Children's Bureau and the Public Health Service approved. The offer of federal matching funds had been tried only once before, in a modest 1914 law to support agricultural extension research, but it would soon enough become utterly commonplace in the United States. The Sheppard-Towner Act provided the template for a dramatically new role for Washington: setting standards for the states and linking federal funds to compliance with those standards.

Sheppard-Towner proved to be controversial, however, and Grace Abbott was its public defender. As the law was set to expire in 1929, she wrote to her father, "I am meeting Miss Lathrop in a few minutes to go over the history of the Washington battle and plan the next engagement. It is in the main guerilla warfare."[22] Like child labor legislation before it, Sheppard-Towner foundered when it faced the need for legislative renewal—though not because of any court ruling.

The administration of Herbert Hoover also objected to an extension of Sheppard-Towner on more than budgetary grounds. President Hoover made it known that he opposed the establishment of a program for children's health "on the shifting sands of overcentralization."[23] He was the last president who believed that the private charitable sector could be the main engine of assistance and uplift for the poor. That unwavering opinion—even as it pertained to emergency financial relief in the teeth of the Depression—would help undo his presidency and undermine his reputation in history. He was surely naive in dismissing the need for financial assistance in a situation of mass unemployment, but in retrospect his views on the importance of separating the state from social services merit renewed attention, especially when it comes to promoting values and norms.

When Hoover convened his White House Conference on Child Health and Protection in 1930, it was the last time a full-throated effort was made by a presidential administration to restrain the growth of social services funded and directed by government. The conference drew three thousand attendees, and its agenda was broad, including problems of dependent children, regular medical examination, school or public clinics for children, adequate milk supplies, maternity instruction and recreation, voluntary organization of children, and child labor. It nonetheless turned out to be a stormy confrontation between two different philosophies on how to address these concerns. On one side were reformers who would use the condition of children as a wedge to open the way for a welfare and social service state; on the other were those, including Hoover himself, who feared the growth of government power in such areas.

The controversy pitted Grace Abbott against an articulate opponent, Ray Lyman Wilbur, the secretary of the interior and a medical doctor. Abbott saw in Wilbur both a bureaucratic and a philosophical antagonist. She believed, correctly, that he wished to transfer the duties of the Children's Bureau to the Public Health Service—hardly an illogical idea, given its ostensible focus on maternal and infant health. She and others such as Lillian Wald, founder of the Henry Street Settlement in New York and among the nation's most admired women at the time, viewed Wilbur's idea as a threat to the very existence of the Children's Bureau. For his part, Wilbur viewed the Children's Bureau, unfavorably, as the cutting edge of a government-led approach to social problems.

Wilbur gave a dramatic keynote address at the 1930 conference, and it turned out to be the swan song of defense for civil society as the primary provider of social assistance and disseminator of norms. He stressed that government must do well in its core responsibility to protect public health, for children and others. This work entailed "inspectors of dairy herds, the inspectors of milk, the promptness of delivery systems, refrigeration, medical advice as to the mixing of formulae, the chlorination of water, the preparation of sugars and grains," and the like. These responsibilities, Wilbur said, "must be in the hands of those who know the reasons for what they do. The indicators of failure to do any part of this task well are the little headstones in the cemetery."[24]

Wilbur also highlighted the public interest in the healthy development of every child. Very much in the tradition of Charles Loring Brace, he offered a paean to the potential of children from all social and ethnic backgrounds, "white and black, yellow and red, rich and poor, and all that lies between." Indeed, he declared, "The wretched frame of a little body may have in it the brain and spirit of a Caesar, a Cicero, a Keats, a Washington, a Steinmetz, a Shelley, a Stevenson, or a Roosevelt. It is not for us to foretell the potentialities of a baby." A proper concern of government was to remove obstacles to the realization of that potential:

We must remember that there are hundreds of thousands of individuals of pre-eminent ability in our population at all times. Many of these are serving us, but others, for lack of opportunity, or lack of self-control, or training, or because of bad habits, the use of drugs, or other ulterior influences, have been blighted. While we must seek out and open up the way for those of superior capacity, we must discard those artificial factors which often curtail full development and which are really under our control.

Pointedly, however, Wilbur cautioned against a "centralization" of efforts to help children realize their potential. The aim must be "to extend and strengthen those community forces which stand to the child in place of many of the earlier responsibilities of home and parents." Government agencies should not try to replace parents, he said: "No one should get the idea that Uncle Sam is going to rock the baby to sleep."[25]

Wilbur's address exemplified the overall tone of the conference, whose message (in Lela Costin's summary) was: "The remedy for child welfare usually required individual initiative, personal reform on the part of parents, the elimination of faults of character, and teaching children to grapple with life."[26]

President Hoover himself emphasized the formative over the reformative in his address to the conference, avoiding mention of a specific role for government:

> From your explorations into the mental and moral endowment and opportunities of children will develop new methods to inspire their creative work and play, to substitute love and self-discipline for the rigors of rule, to guide their recreations into wholesome channels, to steer them past the reefs of temptation, to develop their characters, and to bring them to adult age in tune with life, strong in moral fiber, and prepared to play more happily their part in the productive tasks of human society.[27]

Hoover called on the conference to adopt a Children's Charter, but he emphasized the responsibility of the community, not the government per se. "For every child," he said, there must be "a community which recognizes and plans for his needs, protects him against physical dangers, moral hazards, and disease; provides him with safe and wholesome places for play and recreation; and makes provision for his cultural and social needs."[28]

Grace Abbott delivered remarks with a diametrically opposed emphasis, and going well beyond discussing the condition of children. She spoke more broadly "about unemployment, the inequitable distribution of wealth for children and families, about what low wages cost a community and who paid that cost, about current worldwide unemployment that was causing large-scale suffering among children, and the long-term costs to those children, not only in health, but also in psychological well-being."[29] Civil society, she clearly believed, was simply not up to the task of dealing with these problems.

The style of Abbott's remarks, displaying rhetorical gifts long honed through her public persona, would become familiar in American public discourse: an emotionalized description of social welfare issues, carrying the implication that those who don't think the government should lead the effort to relieve the distress are lacking in compassion. "There are many children tonight who have not known security in their homes for over a year," she said. There are "many families that will not be taken care of by charity this winter where the family standards have gone steadily down...such as to produce almost nothing at all to share. You can never make up to those children for that." She recommended "payments for children" during economic downturns.

Abbott's speech was received with such prolonged applause that the session's chairman had to cut it off. It perfectly enunciated the reformers' strategy of using the situation of children as an emotional lever to move public policy toward social insurance and a role for the state in overseeing social services. Indeed, after retiring from the Children's Bureau in 1934 because of the tuberculosis that would ultimately take her life, Abbott devoted most of her remaining years to writing a two-volume book tellingly titled *The Child and the State*.

Ray Wilbur might be said to have prevailed in the short-term sense that the Sheppard-Towner Maternity and Infancy Protection Act was not renewed. Moreover, the Children's Bureau would remain small. Yet as John Sorenson observed in his introduction to a collection of Abbott's writing, the bureau "prophesied the emergence of a more powerful federal government."[30]

Just five years later, in fact, the social welfare firmament of the United States turned dramatically—and permanently—away from an emphasis on character and morals as prerequisites for upward mobility. The focus shifted toward ensuring at least a modicum of financial security through the booms and busts, the innovation and disruption of the modern economy. The landmark Social Security Act of 1935 powerfully reflected the views of Grace Abbott and her fellow reformers and settlement house alumni—many of whom had come to populate the Franklin Roosevelt administration. One Hull House alumna, Frances Perkins, became the first woman to hold a cabinet position, as secretary of labor. She chaired the crucial Committee on Economic Security, which crafted the Social Security Act. Among its five members was Harry Hopkins, who led the New Deal's Federal Emergency Relief Administration and had begun his career at New York's Christodora House, where he sought to combine public housing and social services. Serving with Hopkins was Henry Morgenthau, the treasury secretary, who had himself founded and financially supported the Bronx House in New York. (Eleanor Roosevelt was friendly with settlement house leaders, including Jane Addams, Lillian Wald, and Mary Simkhovitch of New York's Greenwich House.)[31]

The advisory board of the Committee on Economic Security included Grace Abbott. Though retired from the Children's Bureau, she continued her efforts to advance the idea that social problems could be solved through government action, thus launching the era of Social Security.[32] Abbott worked to "reach the public" as a columnist for the *Chicago Evening Post* and for *Parents* magazine. As a contributor to NBC Radio she was among the first American women to reach a national broadcast audience.[33] *Good Housekeeping* magazine named her one of America's twelve most admired women. She was a powerful voice in persuading Congress to include Aid to Dependent Children in the Social Security Act of 1935.[34]

The Social Security Act, which the historian Blanche Coll has described as an "artful mix of insurance and welfare,"[35] linked the long-building crusades for economic support for the elderly and the unemployed with Grace Abbott's crusade to bring the state into the lives of children through financial support for their families and a range of public health services specifically for mothers and children. Yet neither the social insurance campaigners nor the children's advocates got everything they wanted in the new law. Indeed, something that neither group expected would emerge out of it: the social service state.

The Social Security Act included, of course, old-age assistance (for those in current distress) and insurance for people too old to work, based on individual contributions to the new system but universally distributed by the Social Security Board and a staff of economists. Assistance for those who could not be—or were not—in the labor force was complemented by state-administered (but federally mandated) unemployment compensation payments.

Going beyond the aged and the disabled, the Social Security Act also included Aid to Dependent Children—what Abbott had called "payments for children." A strong case can be made that the Depression, with the pressure it put on government to help those clearly in need, was decisive in moving the federal government to provide financial assistance to single parents and to offer grants for social workers who would enroll households in the program. According to Blanche Coll, the section of the Social Security Act providing for children's services was "little noticed" while the legislation was being framed, and it was "more or less slipped in to round things out."[36] Yet what had been a patchwork of "mothers' pension" programs was now a section in the law that would serve as the foundation of the American social welfare state.

For the first time, and with a congressional appropriation of $24 million, the federal government took the lead in providing "money payments" for dependent children: "those under the age of 16 who [have] been deprived of parental support or care by reason of the death, continued absence from the home, or physical or mental incapacity of a parent." Although this $24 million appropriation was considered relatively meager by its advocates, Harry Hopkins presciently observed that it would grow significantly. (Hopkins preferred public employment programs to ameliorate poverty caused by downturns in the business cycle.)

The Social Security Act included not just individual financial payments for the families of dependent children, but also "grants to states for maternal and child welfare"—essentially the old Sheppard-Towner Act revived and expanded. The Children's Bureau would allot funds to the states after reviewing "a state plan for maternal and child-health service" on the basis of seven distinct criteria, including that they "provide for the development of demonstration services in needy areas and among groups in special need." Such was the new language of federal direction. At first, only small amounts were disbursed, just $2.8 million in a year; but the groundwork had been laid for grants that would total tens of billions annually less than a century later. The projected total expenditure over the coming decade (2019–2028) is in the trillions.[37] This development fit well with Grace Abbott's long-held views on the state's responsibilities to poor children.

But Abbott and like-minded reformers were dealt a blow by the Social Security Act as well. Aid to Dependent Children would not be based simply on a household's financial situation, as they had envisioned, nor would it be part of the Children's Bureau, but would instead be overseen by the Social Security Board. Any household receiving help would have to demonstrate eligibility in a personal interview. Those conducting the investigations would not be accountants checking on financial assets, but professional social workers.

Before long, hundreds of social workers who had been employed by the Federal Emergency Relief Administration began to seek university degrees in social work. Federally funded scholarships directed students to schools of social work across the country, notably the one at the University of Chicago, led by Edith Abbott, which quickly won national recognition and enrolled students from every state. As Costin writes, "Edith Abbott assumed a broker role in the placement of her students in the developing public welfare system." She was thus able to "advance her concept of social work in the public sector by educating and sending out staff all over the country."[38]

So it was that the profession whose pedigree was that of the "friendly visitor" would now be populated by agents of the state. Financial assistance was coupled with casework, provided by public workers, with a focus on the specific problems of individual families. This is what Andrew Polsky calls the "therapeutic state."[39]

Josephine Brown, a professional social worker and advocate for the profession, and a colleague of Harry Hopkins, envisioned social casework as being largely "directed towards the treatment of problems inherent in individuals and families — their inadequacies, their failures, their personality difficulties." She actually wanted to keep financial relief separate from such casework, but once social workers were designated to serve as the ground troops in the Aid to Dependent Children program, the two elements of the social service state were brought together. Brown described that marriage in this way: "We are creating a new type of social work and of public welfare, adapting whatever is applicable from the rest of social work and adding the results of our own experience [in government] in standards, training, methods and terminology."[40]

This new approach to social work might be seen as an effort to reach as many households as possible, or in today's parlance, to "scale up." Private charity was seen to be inadequate for providing assistance to everyone hurt by downturns in the economy. For that matter, one might conclude that supplying all the social workers needed for personal interventions also required the resources of government. The impulse to scale up, to provide something akin to universally available social services through government action, would later be justified by the social scientist Lester Salamon on grounds of what he called "voluntary failure," meaning a failure of the nonprofit sector to fill the full need for social services.[41] Put another way, a nonprofit sector staffed by volunteers was no longer practical.

Of course, advocates of scaling up would endeavor to ensure that government involvement didn't just expand the scope and reach of services, but also delivered uniformly high quality. Perhaps the social work profession was self-confident enough to believe that was possible. One cannot, however, rule out the possibility that professional social workers such as Brown saw, in the depth of the Depression, a means to establish publicly supported employment opportunities in social work—a dramatic change that would become the norm henceforth.

It's hard to imagine that Mary Richmond, the social work pioneer, would have approved of this change. In *Friendly Visiting Among the Poor*, she cautioned strongly against "indiscriminate relief," and later she opposed the public provision of mothers' pensions. She would also have been troubled by the linking of eligibility for aid with the recipient's acceptance of individual counseling, provided by trained professionals rather than concerned neighbors and citizens. This made it all the more difficult, in her thinking, to offer disinterested but pointed help. Most crucially, the necessity of building character was lost, and Richmond saw this as "a common fault of modern philanthropy. Rich and poor alike are pictured as the victims of circumstances of a wrong social order." She cited a political writer of the time remarking that "when our forefathers became dissatisfied, they pushed farther into the wilderness, but . . . now, if anything goes wrong, we run howling to Washington."[42]

Even Edith Abbott, Grace's alter ego, recognized the importance of personal character traits for long-term success. She looked to social work primarily as a vehicle for research about poverty and structuring efficient public welfare administration, through "statute-drafting, administrative law, the court system, and economic principles as they applied to questions of social insurance."[43] To Edith in her role as a university dean, writes Costin, "reality for the poor and disadvantaged and handicapped was reflected in rates of unemployment, in the punitive environment of relief offices, and in the incidence of infant mortality. For her, little more needed to be said."[44] In other words, economic realities were the first line of government effort to support those in need. At the same time, the Abbott view toward statutory reform was actually linked to the sort of Victorian virtues that Mary Richmond endorsed. Speaking at the National Conference of Social Work in 1928, Edith took issue with the Freudian language of "personality" that had become commonplace among social work professionals, and she suggested that some were using that term when they really meant "character." For Edith, character included "honesty, courage, fair and square dealing, respect for human rights and for all human beings even if they are very poor and very troublesome, willingness to make personal sacrifices for a good cause and above all the ability to assume grave responsibility."[45] She was reminding social workers that an emphasis on character remained a potent force for long-term uplift.

American civil society had once sought to reinforce such virtues, but the emerging social service state would focus instead on fixing problems. Reformers scored great victories—old-age income insurance, aid for dependent children, federal aid for state maternal and child health programs—but lost the battle to keep material aid separate from social work as understood in the civil society tradition. Mary Richmond created the model of "casework," or interventions into the individual lives of what Andrew Polsky calls the "marginalized working class." But her idea that such interventions were to be private and "friendly" did not survive the agenda of Abbott's generation, which emphasized behavior modification—often along Freudian lines—and successfully obtained public funding for such work on a large scale, thus gaining long-term government support for career social workers. Going forward, few would look to civil society for the sort of character building once offered by the Newsboys' Lodging House or the kind of neighborhood assistance provided by the early settlement houses. Now, Uncle Sam *was* rocking the cradle.

One can approve of a strengthened system of financial relief for those in dire straits, and assistance to the elderly, and public health programs for pregnant women, but still observe that the shift from formative work by civil society to reformative work by agents of government created a vacuum—the space once filled by promoters of bourgeois norms, such as Charles Loring Brace and the early Jane Addams. Government, by its nature, is a provider of tangible services: emergency financial assistance, foster-care placement, unemployment compensation. These provisions assume, to some extent, that the poor are victims of circumstances beyond their control. Government can't provide the intangible guidance that civil society can offer, such as advice in how to gain control, or agency, over one's circumstances. As Brace and others believed, it is bourgeois norms that empower the poor to rise in a society of opportunity. When government does attempt to promote norms, it oversteps its proper role and creates controversy, as we will see in the following chapter.

Providing services is fundamentally different from promoting constructive norms for personal behavior. Further, the growth of government social services for those in difficulty implies that reformative services are the answer to their problems, and it inevitably attracts concerned and talented people into government with the hope of administering and delivering those services. The shift toward social services and away from the promotion of norms accelerated as government drew civil society into its financial embrace.

A monumental transition had occurred in the few short years between the White House Conference on Child Health and Protection in 1930 and the passage of the Social Security Act in 1935. From then on, the Freudian-influenced social workers and the Progressive reformers were ascendant. The vanquished were those who believed that voluntary local organizations emphasizing character and bourgeois norms could, and must, prepare the poor to strive and succeed, if only modestly. While Edith Abbott's zeal for legislative reform helped carry the day, even she was disappointed in the trend among social workers whom the government was now employing. She feared they were becoming too focused on "case work methods and such phenomena as the ego libido and various psychiatric diagnoses," and too little concerned about their responsibilities in larger matters of public welfare.[46]

The friendly visitors of the nineteenth century saw their role as that of helpful neighbors, aiming "to supply every needy family with a friend," as Mary Richmond put it. In the twentieth century, friendly visiting and secular organizations that promoted constructive social norms, such as the Children's Aid Society and the early settlement houses, were on the wane. The values that guided Mary Richmond's approach to the virtuous intervention of social work would be swept away by government support for a qualitatively different sort of effort.

In *Friendly Visiting Among the Poor*, Richmond emphasized the importance of improving the prospects of the poor, not focusing on their problems. Only a carefully nurtured friendship could, she believed, encourage the habits that enable the disorganized poor (or anyone in difficult straits) to improve their situation. Like Matilda Sternberger, my father's visitor, Richmond believed in the capacity of the poor "breadwinner" to be charitable toward others and to be a force for good in his neighborhood. The friendly visitor, she wrote, "must know how to work with the forces that make for progress...to forward the advance of the plain and common people to a better and larger life."[47] She judged such progress in the most subtle of ways. For example, she describes the "transfiguration" of a woman who had been "quite ordinary," according to a friendly visitor named "Miss Frances Smith," whom Richmond quotes: "Imagine our surprise in finding," four years later, "that a certain dignity and earnestness akin to that of the visitor, had crept into this woman's life, and found expression in her face and bearing."[48] The effort to encourage uplift went far beyond matters of financial need; it was a retail dissemination of social norms that manifest even in a person's spontaneous self-presentation.

Such a result was among the "rewards of friendship," as Miss Smith called them. Those rewards are inconsistent with visiting as an agent of the state—one who represents the possibility of gaining or losing benefits. This is why the passage of the Social Security Act, with its governmental embrace of the social work profession, was so consequential.

It's important to note that the change was not immediate or absolute, as older ways coexisted with the new model of social work. As late as 1929, a new settlement house, Bronx House, was founded in New York. Its main philanthropic support, according to a *New York Times* account, came from Henry and Josephine Morgenthau, identified as the founders. Henry Morgenthau would later become secretary of the treasury and a key shaper of the Social Security Act. At the opening ceremony of Bronx House, he presumably looked on approvingly as one of the speakers observed that while the city was spending $130 million a year on education, "you have here an influence exerting itself far beyond the public school. Here the children come not merely for the development of the mind but also for the flourishment of spiritual health."[49] (Bronx House is still in operation in 2019, emphasizing fitness and health programs and relying on funding from eight government agencies, along with private philanthropy.)

The same year that the Social Security Act was passed, my father, at age eleven, living in a foster home arranged by private charity, continued to be visited regularly by a volunteer in his home above his foster father's barber shop. His visitor described herself as a "social worker" to the Juvenile Aid Society, which was then sending its annual membership fee to the American Association for Labor Legislation, whose cofounder Abraham Epstein coined the term "social security." This snapshot from my own father's experience in the 1930s reveals that change was gradual but clearly moving in one direction: away from civil society providing care and promoting norms, and toward a social service state.

Grace Abbott, after leaving government in 1934, returned to Chicago to take a faculty position at the School of Social Service Administration led by her sister, Edith. The two lived together in a house near the university, with a screened porch where Grace could sleep, which her physician thought would alleviate the symptoms of her tuberculosis.[50] Grace took on the editorship of the *Social Science Review*, which under Edith's leadership had promoted the Children's Bureau worldview. Her health steadily declined until in June 1939, as Edith put it, "she was relieved of her awful struggle to breathe."[51] (Whether Edith's values were Victorian can be debated, but she clearly had a Victorian's way with words.)

Grace had nonetheless managed in 1938 to publish her two-volume magnum opus, *The Child and the State*, a historical documentation of child welfare services from colonial days to the New Deal, including a wide range of primary source material along with her own annotations and commentary. She was thorough and neutral in many of her descriptions, yet clearly conveyed her view that progress in child welfare could be achieved only with a larger role for the federal government, and left no doubt that her focus on child welfare was only the point of entry to a far greater role for government in social welfare writ large.

Abbott expressed the same idea in one of the last major speeches of her life, delivered at a Children's Bureau dinner in April 1937:

Historically, the children or the cause of children has been the spear-
head in the struggle for better economic and social conditions, better
organization of the government for the service of its citizens. . . .
[T]hose who have undertaken to safeguard children must propose
what often seems, at the time, a revolutionary change in the conception of the functions of government, and must experiment with new
administrative and judicial procedures.

Doing so, she continued, "requires a combination of courage and wisdom, of sagacity and opportunism, of patience and of impatience if results
are to be achieved."[52]

Such sentiments are of a piece with a latter-day organization of which
Grace Abbott would surely have approved. The Children's Defense Fund,
founded in 1973 by Marian Wright Edelman, would focus primarily
not on direct aid to children but on legislative goals related to federal
programs, such as those supporting early childhood education, health
care, and tax relief for low-income households. Edelman is one of many
heirs to the legacy of Grace Abbott, who helped bring about a profound
change in American government and its relationship to the poor. Abbott
bridged two eras in starting her work as a resident of a settlement house
with a lingering emphasis on character formation, and then going on to
become one of the architects of the American welfare and social service
state. To the end, she was certain that the gains it offered brought no
losses with them. It is this view that this book disputes.

# 5

# WILBUR COHEN
# AND THE SCALING OF
# THE SOCIAL SERVICE STATE

The growth of the American social service state, the federal government's approach to improving the lives of the poor by funding agencies and hiring agents to implement programs, occurred slowly and incrementally. Public assistance to single parents and related programs for children were only small parts of the Social Security Act, which at its inception was essentially unemployment compensation and old-age assistance. But the die had been cast. The federal government, not the settlement house or the local charity organization society, would be the locus not just of a financial safety net but of "social services" generally.

Few public officials did more to steer the expansion of the social service state than Wilbur Cohen, the consummate federal bureaucrat. The son of an immigrant grocer in Milwaukee, he began his career in 1934 as what his biographer Edward Berkowitz calls "little more than an errand boy" for the Committee on Economic Security, which developed the details of the 1935 Social Security Act. He then proceeded to shape and promote legislation behind the scenes, guided by his own strong views. By 1968, Cohen was at the pinnacle of Washington as secretary of health, education, and welfare in the waning days of the

Lyndon Johnson administration, and known by the nickname "Mr. Social Security."

Cohen served in the federal government for most of his professional career. His life offers a prism through which to view an era of optimism about the capacity of government to satisfy material want and draw the poor into the socioeconomic mainstream. Cohen's ideas about poverty and government led most notably to the 1962 Public Welfare Amendments to the Social Security Act, which would become the foundation for million-dollar programs that turned into multibillion-dollar programs; and those ideas long outlasted his own confidence in them.

Wilbur Cohen's legacy, even more than Grace Abbott's, is based on public policy for the poor, not personal involvement with them. Berkowitz describes both Cohen and his mentor at the Social Security Board, Arthur Altmeyer, as representing "a new breed of reformer" in the history of social policy:

> The comparison with other self-conscious crusaders for social justice, such as Jane Addams and the residents of Chicago's Hull House in the late nineteenth and early twentieth centuries, is instructive.... Jane Addams represented a voluntary tradition of social action, in which few residents of Hull House were paid for their labor, but Altmeyer and Cohen depended on their salaries to make ends meet. Social reform was for them a living as much as it was a calling.[1]

Nor was that their only difference from earlier generations of social reformers. Altmeyer and Cohen were not social workers, nor were they akin to the "friendly visitors" of the past. Instead, they "managed large systems of social welfare that paid benefits as a matter of entitlement." They didn't view social problems at the level of families or communities, but rather in terms of the whole economy.[2]

Cohen, moreover, saw poverty as something to be left behind— though his family was never extremely poor—not something in which to immerse himself by personal interventions among the poor. A paper he wrote at the University of Wisconsin in 1932 gives a scornful description of the Italian neighborhood around Milwaukee's Jefferson Street School, which he attended: "Congestion, filth, dirt, ignorance, uncleanliness, vice, poverty" characterized the place. The city's Third

Ward was filled with "crowded, unpainted, half-tottering bungalows fit for condemnation," and was noteworthy for "the stench of garlic in salami sausage" and for parents who were "unfit for the industrial life of Democratic America."[3]

Cohen, in other words, displayed exactly none of the tolerance—much less enthusiasm—for immigrant neighborhoods that Jane Addams showed. On the contrary, his disdain foreshadowed the sensibility that would drive policies of both the New Deal and the 1960s Great Society: the clearance of neighborhoods judged to be without redeeming value, and taxpayer-supported financial benefits as the primary means of household uplift. Cohen was not involved in the former, but would be central to the latter.

Unlike Addams and Abbott, the young Cohen set his sights on his own upward mobility. His first step up was enrolling in the University of Wisconsin's Experimental College in 1930. The "Ex College" was a tiny de facto honors college where a small group of students lived together and studied a common curriculum of classics for two years. They were exposed, as well, to contemporary political debates in Madison, a hotbed of Progressive legislation on matters that would become part of Cohen's professional portfolio, such as unemployment compensation.[4]

Professional networking, in modern parlance, defined Cohen's undergraduate tenure as much as his course of study, which led him from the Ex College on to a four-year degree in economics. At a time when the Depression had called the efficacy of capitalism into question, Cohen made friends with whom he reflected on the future of the economic system, and some of those friendships would continue when he moved to Washington. Cohen "wished to align himself with definite beliefs and political positions. It would not do to remain indifferent to the nation's problems just because his parents had enough money to send him to school," according to Berkowitz. Cohen himself wrote that "everyone knows we are in a depression," given that "there are close to ten million underemployed at present, women and children are hungry, miners cold and homeless, and panhandlers walking the street." Reflecting on the situation, he concluded that "logic and a development of principles must take the place of laissez-faire."[5] While he took a positive view of the direction that Russia had gone, he wasn't hoping to see the same happen everywhere: "I do not feel that what the world needs is a revolution. I feel that what this world needs is more careful considerations of its present situations and an attempt to better them."[6]

Cohen envisioned himself in a career doing just that. Thanks to being recruited by administrators such as Edwin Witte, whom he'd met in Madison, he became first an expert in social policy and then an administrator of it—roles that would be his ticket from the family business in Milwaukee to legislative signing ceremonies at the White House. Cohen's efforts would lead to government programs that didn't *supplement* private interventions into the lives of the poor, but instead reduced and marginalized them.

The 1935 Social Security Act was the foundation for a federal role in the lives of the poor, and a series of amendments expanded that role— both in the level of financial benefits offered and in the range of social services to be supported by federal funds and matched by state appropriations. The original Committee on Economic Security, to which Cohen was attached and which drafted the Social Security Act, had decidedly not envisioned such a course. The committee members believed that the central feature of the American social welfare state would be social insurance: government-administered pensions for the elderly and unemployment compensation for those out of work, both financed by private contributions from individuals or employers.

The movement for social insurance had been building at least since the publication in 1913 of I. M. Rubinow's landmark book *Social Insurance*, which became the de facto platform of the American Association for Labor Legislation. Rubinow himself served on the Committee on Economic Security, where Wilbur Cohen held his first federal job as an analyst. Rubinow essentially made the case that insurance against unemployment or poverty in old age—unlike the insurance of property—could be provided only through government.

The expectation was that social insurance would be the norm as virtually all Americans were drawn into the workforce, while assistance and relief would fade away. This way of thinking was succinctly expressed by Elizabeth Wickenden, a close friend of Cohen's who was a key part of what he called "the apparatus," an informal group of people both inside and outside government who promoted an agenda of liberal reform. Wickenden, who served as an administrator in the Federal Emergency Relief Administration and later as a lobbyist for the American Public Welfare Association, wrote in a 1945 paper for the organization that "the need for public assistance" could be expected to "be reduced to a minimum through strengthening the social insurance programs."[7]

It was essentially taken for granted that most householders were inclined and prepared to work. The prospect of large and growing rolls of households on cash public assistance, mainly headed by single mothers, was not much contemplated. Nor were social services for such a group anticipated. The leaders of the Federal Emergency Relief Administration, from which architects of social security (including Cohen's mentors) were drawn, believed that economic need did not signal a pathology, and therefore "financial aid was not a tool in treatment, it was *the* tool," as Blanche Coll aptly puts it.[8] In other words, once the financial need was met, nothing more need be offered. Indeed, Wilbur Cohen's first boss at the Social Security Board, Arthur Altmeyer, resisted the hiring of legions of social workers for purposes other than the narrow determination of eligibility for benefits. He went so far as to tell the Congress in 1939 (as per Coll) that "states employed only a few social workers and he expected the situation to stay that way."[9]

It did not. The "caseload" of the Aid to Dependent Children program continued to grow—a fact recognized by internal reports for the federal Bureau of Public Assistance, which administered the program. Leaders commissioned by the bureau to guide its work argued among themselves about their role. A 1943 report discussed "relief as a tool in treatment," while a 1944 report referred to "the right to financial assistance."[10] But there was no doubt that the number of social workers graduating from public universities with an eye toward government service was growing, while their prospective caseload happened to be doing the same. By 1943, Aid to Dependent Children—envisioned as a program for widows or households with incapacitated breadwinners—recorded that 37 percent of its beneficiaries resulted from "estrangement due to divorce, separation, desertion or illegitimacy."

The stage was set for what Coll brands "the welfare mess," leading to a massive expansion of the social service state in the 1950s and early 1960s—an expansion in which Cohen played a central role as he climbed the federal career ladder. His career got a boost when he briefly left government to join the faculty of the University of Michigan School of Social Work from 1956 until 1960 as a full professor of public welfare administration—notwithstanding the fact that he had only an undergraduate economics degree. For the first time, he had a role outside Washington as an independent "action intellectual."[11] It was a brilliant career move, elevating his prestige and influence. Indeed, even his decision to leave Washington did much for his reputation. At a going-away party, Senator John F. Kennedy called him "Mr. Social Security," coining the nickname that became Cohen's sobriquet and the title of his biography.

Cohen's university position brought him recognition as a public figure, poised to shape policy. He was part of the emerging nexus between academia and liberal governance that epitomized the Kennedy years. "Cohen was no longer anyone's surrogate," Berkowitz notes. "He was a figure of intellectual stature who contributed ideas that found their ultimate expression...in the administrations of John F. Kennedy and Lyndon B. Johnson."[12] Cohen articulated an ambitious vision in a 1957 speech in Madison, Wisconsin: "Those of us in social security who were nurtured here in Madison...believe in the idea of progress. We believe that there can be a better life for all. We believe that, for all practical purposes, want can be abolished and poverty eradicated. We believed that human problems are capable of solution."[13]

The backdrop for what would be among the most influential policy roles of Cohen's life—and an extremely consequential one for government social services thereafter—was the postwar explosion of public assistance payments. By 1947, the "welfare boom" had caught the public's attention: $2.3 billion a year in spending despite what *US News and World Report* called "record prosperity." This development stirred up controversy. "Welfare boom stories zeroed in on chiselers and cheats, runaway husbands, live-in boyfriends, unmarried baby breeders, loafers and drunks," as Coll puts it. A December 1947 report by a business group, the Committee on Governmental Efficiency and Economy, concluded that "social work practices fostered continued dependency."[14] Nevertheless, public assistance spending continued to grow, typically because its appropriations were tied to overall Social Security spending, as per the New Deal vision. Federal matching funds increased, in part by a formula designed to provide more for lower-income states. Yet such measures only postponed a welfare crisis; they did not resolve it.

In 1961, it fell to Wilbur Cohen to address the problem from his lofty new perch as assistant secretary for legislation at the Department of Health, Education, and Welfare. Charting a path as a post–New Deal public official, part advocate, part analyst, Cohen regarded members of Congress as his "clients," and outside interest groups as means of influence. He had long worked with his "apparatus" of reform activists, and according to Berkowitz he "shaded the boundary between policy technician and policy advocate." In his first appointed political position, thanks to Abraham Ribicoff, the HEW secretary, Cohen was situated to act as both.[15]

The welfare firestorm that was riveting national attention at the time did not erupt in a big city where poverty was concentrated, but in Newburgh, New York, a small industrial town on the Hudson River. The onetime site of George Washington's military headquarters had become a factory town (making women's purses) and attracted poor African American migrants from the South. There were more migrants—with extended family members—than there were jobs available; nor were the unskilled, undereducated newcomers well prepared for urban life. Because public assistance at the time required localities to pay a substantial share of the cost, Newburgh was spending fully a sixth of its local budget on welfare, more than on police protection.[16]

Soon after taking office as the city manager in 1960, Joseph Mitchell proposed new rules for receiving assistance, such as a work requirement for all "able-bodied males," and Aid for Dependent Children eligibility based on an inspection of the home environment. A Newburgh statute said: "If the home environment is not satisfactory, the children in that home shall be placed in foster care in lieu of welfare aid to the family adults." The new policies stirred up so much controversy that an *NBC White Paper* documentary called it "The Battle of Newburgh."

While Mitchell was a firebrand, he was dispensing public assistance in much the style of the nineteenth- and twentieth-century charity organization societies and their successors: requiring adults to work and placing out children. In my own father's case, the Juvenile Aid Society had been providing assistance to his biological father, but suspended the aid upon reaching the conclusion that he was "shiftless and irresponsible," and then placed my father and his sister in foster care, even before their father's death left them orphaned. The concept of attaching strings to public benefits—an idea with deep philosophical roots in American life—had not been abolished by the New Deal, as Wilbur Cohen would find.

But the new Kennedy administration, under public pressure to deal with rising welfare caseloads of a type never anticipated by the Social Security Act, did not follow the Newburgh playbook to reduce the rolls by attaching conditions to financial aid. Instead, under Cohen's guidance, the philosophy of social insurance would shift toward "services, services," as Blanche Coll succinctly puts it. If those receiving public assistance were not evolving into social insurance contributors on their own, then government would intervene with "rehabilitation" and with "preventive and protective services," intended to "strengthen family life and help individuals attain self-support."[17]

It was an updated version of the New Deal: federally funded social services, delivered by trained caseworkers, designed to usher into the labor force those who otherwise would not be eligible for the social insurance of the Social Security Act. The extremely consequential (but underestimated) 1962 Public Welfare Amendments to the Social Security Act would serve as the foundation of the social service state. President Kennedy described the amendments as constituting "a realistic program which will pay dividends on every dollar invested."[18] Cohen himself called them "the most important changes in the public welfare provisions of the Social Security Act, in that act's history. The amendments emphasize rehabilitation services and the training of staff, liberalize payments, and provide States with significant, new tools for making welfare programs more effective."[19] It was, without doubt, a major change in the way that the federal government provided support for social services. The 1962 amendments also radically changed the relationship between government and civil society.

These changes were assuredly the product of the powerful combination of Wilbur Cohen's vision and his legislative agility. This classic behind-the-scenes bureaucrat even claimed credit, saying, "if it hadn't been for me, there wouldn't have been any '62 amendments. Because neither Kennedy, nor Sorensen, nor Ribicoff, nor Johnson was for it. They would let me do things as long as I took the responsibility."[20] In addition to President Kennedy and Vice President Johnson, he was referring to Abraham Ribicoff (the HEW secretary) and Theodore Sorenson, the key presidential aide and a Cohen confidant.

Cohen was adept in convincing all sides of the debate that the legislation would accomplish their goals: it passed the House 357 to 34, and then the Senate on a voice vote.[21] Well aware of public doubts about welfare, Cohen characterized his efforts in congressional testimony as "waging war on dependency." The weapons of that war would be social services funded by Washington; the troops would be professional social workers. The Bureau of Public Assistance was renamed the Bureau of Family Services. Washington would deliver what President Kennedy promised when he signed the 1962 legislation: "rehabilitation not relief."

It's a deeply revealing phrase. Rehabilitation implies correction, whether of personal failings or actual wrongdoing. Indeed, the law specified failings to be remedied, including "dependency, juvenile delinquency, family breakdown, illegitimacy, ill health, and disability."[22] It's a list of problems that called for reformative, not formative, policy.

The 1962 amendments (informally called the social service amendments)[23] sharply increased federal spending for social services through grants to states, raising the federal share for "services to reduce dependency" from 50 to 75 percent. But that's not the only way the amendments laid the groundwork for the social service state. A crucial element allowed, even encouraged, states to use the federal support to contract with private organizations that previously may not have received government funding. Such contracting was permitted when services "cannot be as economically or as effectively provided by the staff of such State or local agency." They could, instead, be provided through "nonprofit private agencies." What's more, the legislation provided funding for the training of social workers, with the goal that "one third of all persons engaged in social work capacities in public welfare should hold master's degrees in social work."

Thus was birthed the social service state. It may be the nature of government to devise programs for the purpose of alleviating problems—from dependency to family breakdown to juvenile delinquency to illegitimacy—through a panoply of social services. In subsequent years, substance abuse and domestic violence would be added to the list. The foundations had been laid for what would become permanent government programs, directed first by the Department of Health, Education, and Welfare; then by the Administration for Children and Families, the largest division of HEW's successor agency, the Department of Health and Human Services. By 2017, ACF's annual budget was $53 billion.

Cohen had captured the optimism of postwar America and channeled the Kennedy administration's confidence that virtually any problem could be ameliorated by government in such a wealthy and successful country. But it would be an exaggeration to credit him entirely with the 1962 Public Welfare Amendments. Had he attempted to cut back welfare payments drastically—which was the desire of many who viewed them as the source of dependency—the nation's liberal postwar order would not have gone along. The social work industry itself deserves credit for pushing the amendments, as it had grown eager for government support. In order to claim the newly available federal matching funds, state governments were tasked with developing specific plans to reach every child in need, and to employ professional social workers through public or private agencies. States accepting matching funds were required to limit social workers' caseloads to a maximum of sixty, and to maintain a certain minimum number of supervisors.

Government and social services were inextricably intertwined. Indeed, there came to be no difference between civil society and government other than scale and reach—and the sharply different messages each had historically conveyed. And as Mark Stern and June Axinn observe in their social work textbook, the crucial role of public funding for social services "raised questions about the necessity for voluntary agencies at all."[24]

Yet after the passage of the 1962 amendments, the idea that government-sponsored, professionally delivered services would conquer dependency—the long-held New Deal dream—was quickly belied. The 1960s turned out to be an era of welfare explosion, as social services increased along with benefit levels. Between 1962 and 1969, the caseload of Aid to Families with Dependent Children (the new name for Aid to Dependent Children) increased from 3.7 million to 7.3 million, while spending soared from $1.4 billion to $3.5 billion.[25] From 1972 to 1980, AFDC benefits increased by 43 percent (adjusted for inflation).[26]

It was Wilbur Cohen's biggest professional frustration. According to Berkowitz, he "soon realized that the 1962 amendments would not meet their objectives," and later he openly described the legislation as his "greatest disappointment" and a "dismal, 100 percent failure."[27] Yet the programs and their funding streams remained in place.[28] The amendments created a dilemma for the social work profession, some of whose prominent members had insisted that more social services for the poor would improve their family life and thereby decrease the numbers of those receiving public assistance. Instead, the numbers grew rapidly, as did the cost, which raised what Berkowitz calls "embarrassing questions about the effectiveness of social services." One should keep in mind, however, that these questions concerned what was, in effect, a public sector takeover of the "independent sector," the privately supported social service groups in the tradition of Brace, Addams, and Richmond.

What had gone wrong? The answer is important for more than historical reasons, because this model remains operational today: decisions are made at the federal level about how social service funds should be directed; private, nonprofit groups are hired by government to provide those services; professional social workers deliver the services and, perhaps most significantly, attempt to correct specific problems rather than promote positive social norms.

There is a vast difference between the list of values carried by my father's social worker, Mrs. Sternberger—self-respect, self-control, good manners, etc.—and the language of the Public Welfare Amendments, which aimed for "the effective location of deserting parents; the simplification and coordination of administration and operation [to] greatly improve the adequacy and consistency of assistance and related service," and so on. The amendments were intended to "contribute to the attack on dependency, juvenile delinquency, family breakdown, illegitimacy, ill health, and disability," and to "reduce the incidence of these problems, prevent their occurrence and recurrence, and strengthen and protect the vulnerable in a highly competitive world." Where once the emphasis had been positive, it was now negative—reformative, not formative.

No one could argue that the approach of Wilbur Cohen, channeling the optimism of his era, was not well funded. The unprecedented promise of a 75 percent federal share of program spending was meant to seed greater state spending and program participation, which it did. The overall grant money increased from $30 million in 1962 to $50 million in 1969, and was complemented by additional federal funding for new sorts of services such as day care and support for university training of social workers. Day-care funds, as per regulation, must supplement but not supplant any state funding.[29]

Indeed, the money flowed—particularly through what Martha Derthick of the Brookings Institution called "the social services loophole."

Simply put, because Washington was providing guaranteed matching funds, federal spending could increase without limit whenever state spending was increased. State governments quickly realized that for every dollar they spent, they would receive three from HEW. As a result, social service grants-in-aid skyrocketed to an eye-popping total of $1.7 billion by 1972.[30] It was, as Derthick described it, "a gusher of federal funds." Indeed, the White House budget projection for such spending in 1972 "was too low by nearly a billion dollars."[31] All this spending had not been planned either by the president or by Congress, Derthick pointed out. Rather, it was the social work professionals who inspired the decision to offer social services grants.

No credible claim can be made that a failure of the social service profession to achieve its stated goals might be due to insufficient funding: the professionals got all they wanted, and more. As Andrew Polsky noted,

> The 1962 amendments brought social workers into the public spotlight. Under the terms of the legislation, resources would flow into the human service network, lethargic state and local departments would be mobilized, skilled social technicians would be trained for public service, and gaps between agencies would be filled.... [S]ocial personnel had preserved their vision of a casework apparatus encompassing all manner of services for marginal families. The new law seemed to herald the realization of this vision.[32]

The 1962 amendments were supposed to minimize dependency, yet it continued in its sharp upward trajectory. The idea that psychological therapy (rather than moral guidance) would end dependency quite simply failed. Anecdotes about households that were helped—what Polsky calls "happy family stories"—were touted as evidence of success. But when more serious and empirical evaluations were conducted, "it was plain that the therapeutic emperor wore no clothes—casework intervention produced no significant results, no one had studied how clients fared after cases were closed," Polsky writes.[33] With the government involved and the spending spigot opened, "a number of factors combined to subvert the therapeutic project," one of them being that the services and counseling given to aid recipients "bore no relation to the model of therapeutic intervention. Public assistance cases continued to increase, contrary to what proponents of the service strategy had believed would happen."[34]

The flood of public money did much more than allow the expansion of social services; it also changed the vehicles for delivering those services. In their underappreciated study *Nonprofits for Hire: The Welfare State in the Age of Contracting*, the political scientists Steven Rathgeb Smith and Michael Lipsky argue convincingly that government funding radically transformed a sector that formerly "existed outside the government and market spheres," where employees and volunteers had been "free to interact with clients without the pressures of bureaucratic or market accountability."[35] They do not appear to view this as a change for the better. Smith and Lipsky worried that the employees of nonprofit government contractors become, in effect, "street-level bureaucrats" who represent the government, yet are not accountable to any elected official. What once were parallel and complementary worlds—that of the bureaucrat approving a household for financial benefits and that of the community organization helping to improve a neighborhood and the lives of its residents—became utterly intertwined. As a result, the former suffocated the latter. Volunteers became a disadvantage as nonprofits sought to comply with government requirements to hire social workers with master's degrees, whose education in many cases had been supported by government itself.

Not only were the "street-level bureaucrats" tied to the government, but they inevitably brought a different attitude to their work, Smith and Lipsky write—an attitude which helps explain why the social service state would fall short in its mission even as it expanded so much.[36] The social service state had driven out "informal care" based on a personal relationship with those receiving assistance, who are treated as ends in themselves and not as instruments for some other purpose.[37] Organizations involved with the lives of the poor would now have a different set of incentives: to serve as many clients as possible with as many professionals as they can hire; to get new contracts and ongoing revenue by continuing to serve clients, even—or especially—if their problems continue.

The "clients" of the social service state are not likely to be met by volunteers or "friendly visitors" seeking to inspire them and prepare them for self-sufficiency. Instead, they are visited by de facto government employees—at the same time as they are receiving government benefits. There is no obvious place in the government firmament to promote positive norms that lead to a successful life. The government's role is to deal with problems, such as child abuse, lagging cognitive development, or substance abuse. One cannot doubt that some of those employed through the social service state do provide useful assistance— such as referrals to benefit programs, or the removal of children from dangerous homes. But "scaling up" to address a wide range of specific problems overlooks the need for constructive social norms, which are not best—or at all—promoted by government.

In earlier times, the very fact that social elites took a voluntary interest in the poor arguably helped to establish and scale a sense of hope and aspiration, along with other constructive social norms. Spreading a positive message does not require that every person in need of it be visited regularly by a professional social worker. One can well imagine that when Mrs. Sternberger showed up on my father's block in South Philly in her chauffeur-driven black Cadillac, word of her purpose spread quickly through the neighborhood, awakening a sense of higher possibilities.

By comparison, what does the multibillion-dollar budget of the social service state achieve? One way to assess its impact is to track the measures of social health compiled in the *Statistical Abstract of the United States* between 1930 and 2008, as well as the *Historical Statistics of the United States*. One cannot blame the social service state for the trends below, but one *can* say that since 1960 it has failed to slow the decline of marriage, the increase in divorce, the astounding upsurge in out-of-wedlock births, the shrinking of church membership, or the sharp rise in drug overdoses.

The "helping professions" convinced themselves of something that turned out to be untrue: that casework based on the clinical treatment of specific social problems was so likely to succeed that government should spend hundreds of millions of dollars to scale up such enterprises. The private models of civil society were cast aside as antediluvian relics of a less-enlightened era. Indeed, the typical social work textbook adopts a distinctly whiggish tone, granting respect to older models only as foreshadowers of the "need" for government support.

The spending spigot would remain wide open despite the failure of the social service state, which took on new roles for itself: not seeking to urge the poor upward, but instead advocating for greater financial benefits. If the poor were not to be blamed for their situation, the fault had to

| Criterion | 2008 | 2000 | 1990 | 1980 | 1970 | 1960 | 1950 | 1940 | 1930 |
|---|---|---|---|---|---|---|---|---|---|
| *Marriage rates per 1,000 population* | 7.1 | 8.3 | 9.8 | 10.6 | 10.6 | 8.5 | 11.1 | 12.1 | 9.1 |
| *Divorce rates per 1,000 population* | 3.5 | 4.1 | 4.7 | 5.2 | 3.5 | 2.2 | 2.6 | 2.0 | 1.6 |
| *Out-of-wedlock births as percent of total* | 40.6 | 33.2 | 26.6 | 18.4 | 10.7 | 5.3 | 3.9 | 3.5 | |
| *Percent of population in a church or other religious body* | 51 | 57 | 63 | 59 | 64 | 64 | 58 | 49 | (1931) 48.2 |
| *Drug arrests per 100,000 population* | (2009) 538 | 625 | 448 | 256 | 269 | 25.5 | 12.0 | 1.5 (persons sent to prison, not arrested) | 1.4 (persons sent to prison, not arrested) |
| *Drunkenness and liquor law arrests per 100,000 population* | 383 | 472 | 654 | 711 | 1250 | 1396 | | | |
| *Child abuse reports per 1,000 population* | (2009) 2.5 | 3.1 | 2.7 | 3.5 | | | | | |

*Sources:* Various editions of the *Statistical Abstract of the United States* and *Historical Statistics of the United States, Colonial Times to 1970.*[38]

lie with capitalism, whose ill effects must be mitigated. This is the Marxist perspective behind the influential 1971 book *Regulating the Poor: The Functions of Public Welfare* (an expansion of a 1966 article in *The Nation*) by the sociologists Frances Fox Piven and Richard Cloward. They argued that social welfare policies historically were not in the best interests of the poor—either in the levels of relief offered or in the animating attitudes—but instead were a strategy to maintain the poor at a minimal level as a surplus labor supply until the economic cycle demanded them once again. Concerning financial relief programs, Piven and Cloward asserted that "the historical pattern is clearly not one of progressive liberalization; it is rather a record of periodically expanding and contracting relief rolls as the system performs its two main functions: maintaining civil order and enforcing work."[39] The idea that those who were guiding social welfare efforts might have had the best long-term interests of the poor in mind is simply dismissed outright.

Piven and Cloward, atypically for authors of academic work, helped inspire a movement. The National Welfare Rights Organization, led by George Wiley, an African American former chemist, mobilized recipients and potential recipients of public assistance in mass marches and demonstrations, pressing for an increase in the level of benefits and for an expansion of the rolls.

The belief that poverty is to be remedied with generous monetary aid came to characterize the agents of government. It is illustrated in a powerful 1976 *New Yorker* article by Susan Sheehan titled "A Welfare Mother," documenting—in great, nonjudgmental detail—the daily life of a New York City household on public assistance, along with the written impressions of a long series of caseworkers who were then still required to make regular home visits. Sheehan gave a clear view of the multitudinous ways the public assistance system supported a woman with nine children by three men, only one of whom she had married.

Upon immigrating to New York, "Carmen Santana" had gotten work in a leather goods factory and pooled her resources with a common-law husband, also employed, who fathered three of her children. But once she heard about the possibility of public assistance, she applied for it. "Between 1961 and 1966, the semi-monthly checks slowly increased," Sheehan wrote. Then Santana stopped working in 1968, and the checks got much bigger. Sixteen caseworkers were aghast at the physical condition of the household: "the broken front doors and mailboxes, the overloaded electric sockets, the lopsided stoves with no oven doors, the rodents crawling in and out of holes, the dimly lit and grubby hallways, the cracked bathroom ceilings, the cockroaches and insects, the odors in the air." They noted that the Santana children were "rather destructive" and had done considerable damage to walls and floors. In the spirit of the friendly visiting tradition, suggestions were made, as a caseworker recorded: "We also pointed out to Mrs. Santana her need to clean the stove and advised her how she could clean the burners. . . . We suggested to the family that they wash the refrigerator using baking soda or some other solvent cleaner."

According to Sheehan, "If anything distressed the caseworkers more than Mrs. Santana's 'very sloppy' housekeeping, it was her failure to get her children to school regularly." Santana's fifteen-year-old son dropped out of school and became a heroin addict. Her thirteen-year-old daughter dropped out too after becoming pregnant, and the household's public assistance check increased after the birth of the baby. At one point, a fire forced the family out of their apartment—one of a series they lived in.[40]

The caseworkers did not question whether this once-independent household had in fact been drawn into dependency and needed to escape it. Rather, they wrote that the public benefits were inadequate. One caseworker found that Santana was one of a dozen of his clients who "cheat" public assistance while earning income informally (Santana ran numbers; others sold cosmetics door to door). He did not report the fact. "You can't stop the cheating until you give people decent grants," he said. "Welfare grants haven't kept up with inflation in recent years, so a lot of the cheating today is justified."

The contrast with Mary Richmond's original view of social work—or, for that matter, the original mission of the YMCA, the Boy Scouts, the settlement house movement, or the Juvenile Aid Society—could not be more striking. In *Friendly Visiting Among the Poor*, Richmond stressed that assistance should be a "ladder," not a "crutch," and financial aid must therefore be conditioned upon efforts toward self-improvement:

> Our plans must not ignore the family resources for self-help. The best charity work develops those resources. If outside help is needed, it should be made conditional upon renewed efforts at work or in school, upon willingness to receive training, upon cleanliness, or upon some other development within the family that will aid in their uplifting. All this is suggested not with a view to making the conditions of relief more difficult, but with a view to using relief as a lever; ... we should make our help a ladder rather than a crutch, and every sensible, reasonable condition is a round in the ladder.[41]

Social workers offering help should think beyond "the present emergency" that the family was facing, Richmond continued. "We must have a view to the future of the family, and must think not only of what will put them out of immediate need, but of what is most likely to make them permanently self-supporting."[42] As an example of a charity that followed these principles, she named the Hebrew Benevolent Society of Detroit, which did not offer aid to families in which the children were sent to work rather than to school.[43]

Richmond did not shrink from making such help conditional. Indeed, she worried that financial relief could undermine the efforts of others to encourage self-reliance. She cautioned that assistance given to one family might raise unrealistic hopes for material help among other families, and thus it might be "unfair and even cruel." It was important to be "just as well as merciful."[44] What the poor needed most, and deserved, was preparation to meet economic challenges, to achieve independence and upward mobility. Social workers must "know how to work with the forces that make for progress." They should be "working with the democratic spirit of the age to forward the advance of the plain and common people into a better and larger life."[45]

While Richmond strove to foster the norm of independence, her latter-day successors would instead encourage dependence. Forgotten was the optimistic belief of Charles Loring Brace that anyone of modest means who adhered to the right norms—what he called "moral machinery"[46]—could make his way:

> The children of the poor are not essentially different from the children of the rich; the same principles which influence the good or evil development of every child in comfortable circumstances will affect, in greater or less degree, the child of poverty. Sympathy and hope are as inspiring to the ignorant girl, as to the educated; steady occupation is as necessary for the street-boy, as the boy of a wealthy house; the prospect of success is as stimulating to the young vagrant, as to the student in the college.[47]

Somehow, this confidence in healthy norms and in the capabilities of the poor gave way to a resigned pessimism, an unwillingness to make demands or expect the best, and an expectation of long-term dependency, which should at least be made comfortable. The idea that benefits should be enough to live on indefinitely reflected the view that structural failures in the American economic system made dependency inevitable.

Whereas Mary Richmond, like Brace or Lillian Wald, aimed to equip the poor to succeed in the American economic and social system, a good many of their heirs have seen their role as one of confronting that system. This mindset is expressed in "A Marxist View of Social Work," an essay that first appeared in 1972 in the journal *Social Work*, a publication of the National Association of Social Workers, and was reprinted in a book of readings used in graduate programs of social work. The author, Robert

Knickmeyer, argued that social workers should not hold themselves as representatives of a higher social class, but rather *identify with* their clients for a common political purpose:

> Social service agencies for low-income people are controlled by the upper class, which not only creates many socioeconomic problems but also determines what services are provided. These agencies will become responsive to the needs of their clients only when social workers identify with and organize, together with their clients, to assume democratic control of them.[48]

Four decades later, a similar viewpoint appeared in *Days in the Lives of Social Workers: 58 Professionals Tell "Real-Life" Stories from Social Work Practice* (2012). One of those professionals, Asherah Cinnamon, director of the East Tennessee Chapter of the National Coalition Building Institute, describes herself as a "social change agent," battling the ills of society: "The most satisfying part of the work is being able to do something effective and positive about the problems of racism, sexisms, classism, anti-Semitism and all the other 'isms.' I am able to do the work that has my heart and get paid to do it. As a social change agent and community organizer, I get to be involved with a wide variety of people working toward systemic change."[49] This is a long way from taking satisfaction in one's client becoming more like oneself, or introducing the poor to a better class of Americans.

To be sure, many of the social workers telling their "real-life" stories worked in nursing homes, hospices, hospitals, and military bases, bringing cheer and advice to people in difficult personal situations. Some were attempting to mitigate antisocial behavior. For example, a prison social worker recounts efforts to persuade men convicted of assaulting women that they needed to "face their situations honestly and make decisions about living nonviolent lives." But the author also writes of trying to change the "system," rather than defending its virtues and preparing individuals to thrive in it. The prison social worker reveals "how torn I am between the clinical social work I practice daily and the political social work I know needs to be done," and adds, "My work with social justice groups is important to me and provides me with the hope of systemic change."[50] Promoting the idea that the poor face an unjust socioeconomic

and political system is not likely to motivate someone to make the effort
to succeed in it, to say the least.

Even though Wilbur Cohen's vision of deploying social services as
a way to reduce dependency was abandoned by many in the field, the
rushing stream of federal funding continued to swell. This is a familiar
pattern in government, as the economist Bryan Caplan has observed. He
sees it as an illustration of "what psychologists call social desirability bias:
just doing things that sound good whether or not they actually work very
well and not really asking hard questions about whether things that sound
good will work out very well in practice."[51] Notwithstanding Cohen's own
disappointment, the Department of Health and Human Services was re-
organized in 1991 to create the Administration for Children and Families,
the direct successor to the Children's Bureau of 1912. ACF would become
the nerve center of the social service state, dedicated to promoting "the
economic and social well-being of families, children, individuals and
communities through a range of educational and supportive programs
in partnership with states, tribes, and community organizations." It
would disburse grants to the states for "child support enforcement, child
welfare, child care, family assistance, Native American assistance, refugee
resettlement," and a variety of additional social services. By 2014, ACF
was disbursing no less than $53 billion in federal funding, much of it to be
matched by state spending, as Cohen intended—and as Martha Derthick
tracked with alarm. ACF itself boasts that its budget is "larger than whole
cabinet agencies like the Department of Justice, Department of Interior,
and the Treasury Department."

The Administration for Children and Families does not entirely
discount the possibility of the poor bettering their lot. It claims that it
seeks to "empower families and individuals to increase their economic
independence and productivity." But its mission statement emphasizes
problems to solve rather than a positive message of progress. ACF aims to
"improve access to services" in order to "address the needs, strengths and
abilities of vulnerable populations including people with developmental
disabilities, refugees and migrants." Some goals can be described as vague
at best, but clearly emphasize the belief that socioeconomic and political
systems are somehow to blame for the problems of client households,
rather than steering them toward the means and behavioral norms to
improve their own situation. The goals in 2014, for instance, included

"Support Underserved and Underrepresented Populations," as well as "Upgrade the Capacity of the Administration for Children and Families to Make a Difference for Families and Communities," which reads like a mission to obtain yet more funding.

In both tone and substance, this is a world away from Charles Loring Brace, circa 1859, as he reflected on "pauper and vagrant children and their families." Policy toward that population must, he wrote, include "reward for good conduct, success for industry, hope and applause for honesty and virtue, and pain and loss and disapprobation for idleness and dishonesty and vice."[52] Elaborating further on what was needed for the moral uplift of poor children, he wrote:

> The child must have sympathy, individual management, encouragement for good conduct, pain for bad, instruction for his doubts, tenderness for his weakness, care for his habits, religious counsel and impulse for his peculiar wants. He needs, too, something of the robust and healthy discipline of every-day life. He ought to be tried; he ought to labor with a motive; he also should have something of the boundless hope which stimulates so wonderfully the American youth.[53]

This sort of optimism for the uplift of disadvantaged children faded, ironically, as the United States became vastly more prosperous. Meanwhile, the 1962 amendments to the Social Security Act—Wilbur Cohen's legacy—ensured funding for social services beyond the wildest dreams of Brace, who relied on solicitations to his fellow New York citizens. By statute, billions of dollars in ACF funding leveraged additional funds through state matching grants, disbursed to nonprofit organizations; this is "the welfare state in the age of contracting," as Steven Smith and Michael Lipsky called it.

This model has, to be sure, come under philosophical challenge by thinkers who have aimed to revive civil society as the agent of social uplift. Peter Berger and Richard John Neuhaus, writing for the conservative American Enterprise Institute in 1977, drew attention to the idea of "mediating institutions"—churches, community groups, and voluntary associations of all kinds—as key to binding society and helping those in need. Later, President George H. W. Bush endeavored to promote the "thousand points of light" constituting civil society. Yet the new focus on "mediating institutions" did not result in trimming back the social service state; instead, it expanded the range of groups receiving government revenue. "Such was the conceptual confusion that many of the Bush-honored 'points of light' were government grantees," wrote James Pinkerton in 1996, reflecting on the Berger-Neuhaus work. Pinkerton quotes a former Reagan aide saying, "The same politicians who got government money for groups lobbied to get those groups named as points of light, which in turn credentialed them to get still more government money."[54] Pinkerton was reduced to celebrating the fact that federal support for child care would take the form of a tax credit rather than more public institutions.

Writing in a similar vein, William Galston, domestic policy advisor to President Bill Clinton, called for reordering "the relationship between government and the institutions of civil society" in a way that would "enable the public sector to strengthen rather than strangle the voluntary sector." Galston believed that government, in "limited circumstances," might "act directly to invigorate local groups," but he had doubts "that government can select wisely among voluntary sector claimants for public support or that these institutions would be well served by any such 'top-down' strategy." He suggested alternatives such as "vouchers and tax incentives that would allow individuals to strengthen local associations they regard as particularly effective."[55] In other words, Wilbur Cohen's social service state would be revisited only as far as its funding mechanisms were concerned. The core ideas—that social services were the best route to helping the poor and that government should fund them—were intact.

Pinkerton went no further than saying that "few would argue [against] Berger and Neuhaus's basic proposition: that mediating structures can be the agencies of a new empowerment. The great question now is whether such devolutionary change can come fast enough to save American civilization from a miniaturized, globalized whirlwind."[56]

Later evidence has not been encouraging. For example, the administration of President George W. Bush undertook to include "faith-based groups" as recipients of social service funds. Whether this policy is effective in particular instances or not, it cannot but be seen as an acknowledgment—indeed, an expansion—of the social service state. One administration official charged with implementing the policy recorded his intense disappointment in a memoir, *Tempting Faith: An Inside Story of Political Seduction.* "I have seen what happens when well-meaning Christians are seduced into thinking deliverance can come from the Oval Office, a Supreme Court chamber, or the floor of the United States Congress," wrote David Kuo. "They are easily manipulated by politicians who use them for their votes, seduced by trinkets of power and tempted to turn a mission field (politics) into a battlefield."[57]

Expanding the range of grant recipients to include "faith-based" or-ganizations certainly did not rein in the reach and breadth of the social service state. By 2012, an Urban Institute study found that "governments paid close to $81 billion to human service nonprofit organizations for ser-vices through contracts and grants."[58] These included "200,000 contracts and grants with about 30,000 human service organizations," which held an average of seven such contracts (or a median of three). It is worth noting that this flood of social service spending and provision for the "vulnerable" did not prevent the emergence of deeply troubling new social trends, notably a wave of opioid-related deaths. As tracked by the National Institute on Drug Abuse, such deaths increased from 8,000 in 1999 to 70,000 in 2018.[59]

The social service state is, in practice, a far-reaching bureaucracy whose leadership is inevitably distant from those in need. The ACF leadership is tasked with crafting or reviewing detailed grant language for sixty-four individual programs. Officials are always concerned that crises for which they will bear responsibility might erupt far afield.

An insider's view of this problem comes from Daniel Schneider, who headed the Administration for Children and Families from 2006 to 2008.[60] As an example, he cites the grants issued by the Office of Refugee Resettlement to fund thirty-six refugee centers across the country. He hoped they were doing a good job helping families find work and places to live—but also worried about accounts he heard of children released, in corrupt bargains, to "family members" who might actually be sex traffickers. Schneider recalls tension between federal oversight officials and local politicians who wanted to keep grant monies flowing to local nonprofits, even if evaluations found them to be ineffective or worse. He saw loopholes in programs such as the Social Services Block Grant, which allows local officials with pet projects to choose a box marked "other" among the list of sanctioned programs. Schneider was frustrated by sac-rosanct programs such as Head Start, a 1960s-era early-learning program for disadvantaged children that had shown little or no lasting positive effect on educational achievement, according to a series of rigorous social science evaluations. ACF officials have occasionally closed a handful of the worst Head Start centers, but the program as a whole has continued because of deep congressional support, premised on its goals rather than its accomplishments.

The lines of supply and oversight for Head Start, like any other ACF program, are long and thin. The agency is vast and sprawling, as its website makes clear:

> The Administration for Children and Families is comprised of 21 offices including the Office of Regional Operations, which represents 10 regional offices around the country. Each office is specialized in its mission, supporting a variety of initiatives that empower families and individuals and improve access to services in order to create strong, healthy communities. Our programs fund a variety of projects from Native American Language Preservation to Refugee Resettlement to Child Care.[61]

The services provided by all these ACF offices are of a kind once funded and delivered locally, and overseen by local citizens on local boards of directors who were accountable for the results. That model has been supplanted by one in which more households may receive services, but there is good reason to be skeptical that they are being helped. For instance—a very serious instance—a reliable flow of funds from taxpayers has not led reliably to better lives for abused or neglected children.

The social service state, through key nodes such as ACF, directs a substantial portion of its overall budget to child protective services: $98 million in 2017 alone toward the prevention of child abuse, and another $325 million toward child welfare generally. And yet "the American child welfare system is still a frustrating, dysfunctional system that cannot ensure that the children who most need protection will be safe," concludes Richard Gelles, a four-decade veteran in the field.[62] A longtime dean of the School of Social Policy and Practice at the University of Pennsylvania, and holder of the Joanne and Raymond Welsh Chair of Child Welfare and Family Violence, Gelles documents a long string of children's tragic deaths caused by their abusive parents or dangerous foster situations—

in New York, Los Angeles, Philadelphia, and North Dakota—in his book *Out of Harm's Way: Creating an Effective Child Welfare System.*[63] In a summary of his findings, he writes, "Government has responded to tragedies with more funding and increases in staff, forming blue-ribbon commissions, replacing administrators, reorganizing agencies, and even changing the names of agencies—but there are no significant changes in the capacity to protect children and ensure their well-being."[64]

Gelles believes that the child welfare system is too "parent-centered" and that orphanages have been unwisely ruled out for children in abusive or inadequate homes. Perhaps too much emphasis has been placed on keeping children and parents together. In the era before Washington-based grant-making and "government by contract," local organizations, whether secular or religious, used a variety of approaches, and they had to answer to those who were personally supplying the funds. The aim to provide assured funding for social services—the vision of Grace Abbott and Wilbur Cohen—has led to a point where one of the nation's most deeply versed experts in the field actually *despairs* about the state of child welfare.

Abbott and Cohen made a crucial mistake. It was their belief—particularly Cohen's—that the full range of a household's problems could be remedied by solutions devised in Washington, and that those whose problems were keeping them from the workforce would eventually become employed. If they subsequently became unemployed again, or when they retired in old age, their economic needs would be met by social insurance (Social Security). That assumption was behind the creation of the Administration for Children and Families, a tentacle of the Social Security Act.

Until his death in 1987, Wilbur Cohen remained committed to the idea of social insurance as the key to social welfare. Although he left government in 1969 for an academic appointment at the University of Michigan School of Education—and later took a position at the LBJ School of Public Affairs, University of Texas—he continued to play a leading role in what he called his "apparatus" of interest and lobbying groups, formalized in 1979 under the name "Save Our Security." He continued to focus on the details of Social Security finance, opposing a plan in 1983 to increase individuals' contributions to the fund. This reform would be widely credited with putting the system's financial house in order, but it was not a policy that the heir to Wisconsin Progressivism wanted.

Moreover, the changes that Cohen had set in motion in 1962, leading to the vast growth in social welfare spending, had antiprogressive political consequences. Richard Nixon's election to the presidency in 1968 reflected, in part, "a backlash against the social welfare legislation" passed during the Johnson administration, as Berkowitz writes. Voters had been learning of massive increases in welfare spending, for example in New York City, where the relief rolls were approaching a million people.[65] Ironically, Nixon proposed an expanded social benefit of which Cohen very much approved: the Family Assistance Plan, which would have offered a federally funded income supplement to all low-income families, including two-parent households. The plan, dubbed "Nixon's Good Deed," failed in significant part because the political Left thought it insufficiently generous. The political Right opposed it for being too generous, and for potentially encouraging dependency instead of work. Its passage in the House of Representatives—before stalling in the Senate—represented the pinnacle of Wilbur Cohen's aspirations.

Given the severe economic upheavals that have marked the modern era, it is difficult to argue against benefits for the unemployed or income supplements for those earning low wages. There are reasonable debates over whether social welfare benefits are appropriate or necessary in an industrial democracy, and whether they should be conditional (on work) or limited (by time period). But these benefits have not just supplemented people's incomes; they have substituted for what Joel Schwartz calls the "moral uplift" and "norms promotion" once offered by Charles Loring Brace, Mary Richmond, and Josephine Shaw Lowell. Schwartz argues convincingly that "we need not choose between two mutually exclusive alternatives, with the poor being either wholly responsible for their condition (hence in need of nothing but moral reformation) or wholly unable to remedy it (hence in need of nothing but material assistance)."[66] Moral uplift can and should coexist with material aid.

Today there is a vacuum where the optimistic promotion of bourgeois norms for success once thrived. Government at various levels has sought to fill the vacuum, but these efforts have been controversial and often short-lived. A different approach is clearly needed, and as the next chapter illustrates, some individuals are stepping up to the task.

# 6

# GEOFFREY CANADA'S REVIVAL OF "MIDDLE-CLASS VALUES"

I n New York, where Charles Loring Brace once sought to inspire newsboys, a native of the impoverished South Bronx set out more than a century later to build a structure of civil society that could promote healthy social norms in Manhattan's famously poor Central Harlem. Geoffrey Canada followed the path charted by Brace in many ways: He focused on children who were not yet in trouble, and were still of an age to choose an upwardly mobile path to middle-class life. He would emphasize the formative, not the reformative. He did not seek to reform the institutions of the day, but to work in parallel with them, arguably transcending them.

Geoffrey Canada's privately funded "Harlem Children's Zone" started in the 1990s with one block that was plagued by drug dealing and violence, gradually expanding to cover 119 Harlem blocks. He first reached dozens of children, eventually tens of thousands. Given the successes of the Harlem Children's Zone, it is understandable that the federal government would attempt to apply the model across the country. This effort, however, served to demonstrate anew the limits of government in promoting social norms, and in this respect the story of the Harlem Children's Zone encapsulates the history of American social services.

Perhaps no one would have appeared more unlikely to revive the tradition of Charles Loring Brace than Geoffrey Canada. He was raised in the starkest possible contrast to Brace, who was the son of rural Connecticut gentry, spurred by religion to uplift the poor. While Brace was attending Yale and writing tracts against slavery, Canada's ancestors were enslaved in North Carolina. Canada was himself raised by people whom Brace would have viewed as part of the "dangerous classes," and his childhood was marked by poverty, violence, and life on the street.

Born in 1954, Geoffrey Canada was one of four children raised by a single mother so poor that she "moved her young children from one cramped apartment to another, trying to stay ahead of the rent and the bills...feeding her boys with rice and beans and powdered milk and government-surplus cheese and government-surplus peanut butter." His father had abandoned the family, "vanished into drink and dissolution. He never sent a dollar to help raise his boys. He never even sent a birthday card."[1]

In a memoir starkly titled *Fist Stick Knife Gun: A Personal History of Violence*, Canada recounts his adolescence on Union Avenue in the Bronx and the street violence into which he found himself drawn—first as an observer, then as a participant. One incident involved a neighborhood interloper who had taken a ball belonging to one of Canada's friends after it had struck the man's car. The friend confronted the man.

> Mike took a step to the man's left. He spoke with unmistakable conviction.
>
> "Listen, if you don't give me my ball, I'm gonna kick your fucking ass right now all up and down this block."...There was no doubt a vicious fight was about to ensue....
>
> The man pulled out his car keys and took a step toward the trunk of his car. We all knew that some men carried their guns in their trunk....
>
> Mike's hand went into his pocket and we could all hear the click of the knife locking....Junior put his hand inside his jacket at his neck, where I knew he often wore a chain with a combination lock on it, a dangerous weapon. Both of them stepped toward the man. If he thought he was going to scare them off he was mistaken. This was their block.[2]

The interloper backed down—but that was hardly the norm on Union Avenue. Canada wrote of his own repeated confrontations:

> By the time I reached the sixth grade, it was recognized by all the tough boys in school that not only would I fight but I knew *how* to fight....Anyone who "messed" with me knew that they would get a "hard way to go," meaning...they would get no quick and easy victory in either a verbal confrontation or a physical one.[3]

It wasn't just a readiness to fight that characterized the culture of Union Avenue and similar neighborhoods. "Many of the children of America are conditioned early to kill and, more frighteningly, to die for what to an outsider might seem a trivial cause," Canada observes.[4] He understands this recklessness as a result of "seeing no way out."[5] It was not that there really was no way out, but most of his peers could not see it. They disdained academic success, a way to a better life, and this created a problem for "Geoff" when he was placed in P.S. 99's "special progress classes." His peers, he wrote, assumed that there was an "inverse relationship between intelligence and ability to fight. Everyone assumed that those in the 'smartest' classes couldn't fight and those in the 'dumbest' classes could."[6]

Geoff had found that he needed to fight. But the central struggle of his adult life would be to change the culture so that anger and violence— rooted in hopelessness and jealousy—would no longer be the norm. He survived Union Avenue and became an apostle to the African American poor, bringing a hopeful message of "middle-class values," as he unapologetically called them.

Central Harlem was historically one of New York's poorest neighborhoods, marked by high rates of incarceration, academic failure, and an array of interrelated social problems. Canada bluntly labeled it a "black hole for tax dollars," as it drew in social service programs for foster care, drug-use rehabilitation, employment training, and "welfare" cash assistance—but generated little in the way of tax revenue. In short, it was an unproductive neighborhood. Canada's alternative vision was what he called, with intentional irony, "contamination, in which positive ideas and practices spread within a family and throughout a neighborhood."[7]

In a sense, Canada's vision grew out of "positive contamination" from his own mother, the former Mary Williams. She was herself the product of a strict upbringing in a two-parent family, and the first in her extended family to attend college—in North Carolina for two years, until family funds were exhausted and she returned to the South Bronx. A failed marriage left her with four children to raise on her own, but she didn't forget her interrupted education or discount its value. She was "still pining for her lost college years, and she bombarded her sons with books and educational experiences before they could even walk," writes Paul Tough in his portrait of Canada and his project.

> She would read *Tom Swift* adventure stories to young Geoff and his brothers every night and by day take them to the library and the Bronx Zoo and the Museum of Natural History.... She had grown up in the strict values of the striving black working class [and] did something that very few welfare mothers in the Bronx were doing in the 1950s and 1960s: she passed on her parents' aspirational values to her own children.[8]

The formative values of Geoff's early years were "race-conscious and proud, devoted to the block and the neighborhood but also focused on success, learning, working hard, getting to college."[9]

As a high school student, he lived with his mother's parents in the predominantly black suburban town of Wyandanch, Long Island. There, at the public Wyandanch High School, he became president of the senior class, captain of the football team, and a member of the drama club. An unlikely chain of events initiated by civil society brought him to Bowdoin College, the elite, private, old New England liberal arts school. The Long Island chapter of the Prince Hall Masons, the so-called "black Masons," offered scholarships to high-achieving black students, and Canada was chosen to receive one without having to apply for it. A white guidance counselor encouraged him to apply to Bowdoin, which was under pressure from white civil rights activists to admit many more black students than it ever had. So it was that Geoffrey Canada arrived in Brunswick, Maine—a black man in a small sea of white faces for the first time in his life.

He found his way among the white and wealthy at Bowdoin, making connections that would later prove useful when he set about to do philanthropic fundraising. More crucially, the vivid impression that Bowdoin's character made on him became a direct catalyst for his life's work, for he saw in practice a set of cultural norms radically different from his childhood environment:

> At Bowdoin we never saw a police officer, ever in the four years I was on the campus of Bowdoin. There was a sense of sort of order, of focus of purpose, sort of permeated the place and you could feel it as soon as you hit the campus. And it was so dissimilar from going back to the South Bronx.

The idea that this sense of order and purpose could become the norm in a disorganized and impoverished black ghetto—that a poor neighborhood need not be a bad neighborhood—did not come to Canada suddenly. A series of experiences sparked his insight that social norms are not innate or specific to a demographic group.

Following his graduation from Bowdoin, he earned a master's degree at the Harvard Graduate School of Education, then became a counselor at a school for violent adolescents in Boston. They were mostly tough and impoverished Irish and Italian Americans from South Boston and Charlestown neighborhoods that were far more like the South Bronx than he would ever have expected.

> I knew black poverty. I saw the impacts of what was happening. I saw the chaos in families. I saw parents who really had no idea what to do with their kids. They didn't really know how to raise their kids. They had their own issues. They were drinking and there was drugs. And kids were growing up in this chaos. I saw that in the South Bronx. But then I began to see it in these housing projects with all white kids and families. And for me, now I'm 24, this was unbelievable. Why? Because I had never seen it. I had never experienced it. I had never been around white people. I mean, the white people at Bowdoin were all like upper-middle-class kids. They didn't have those kinds of problems. So, now I'm looking at these kids from Charlestown and from South Boston; tough Italian and Irish kids who were just like the kids I grew up with in the South Bronx. And it said to me something else was going on here. And there was something about a set of beliefs.

Dysfunctional cultures and their attitudes, he realized, were not delimited by race—nor, conversely, did race make such attitudes inevitable.

He was struck by the implicit values of the poor white cultures he encountered and their similarity to those that characterized the South Bronx of his childhood.

What did the kids believe in all places? They believed that they were not wanted. And they believed that the world was kind of unpredictable and dangerous. They believed that the escape you could get was short-term and it usually came in a bottle or a pill, or some other form of what they would consider to be release. And they believed there was no way to get out. You couldn't get out. That in the end you were trapped there. Almost invariably the families were chaotic and very troubled. There was substance abuse. There was child abuse. There was a lack of education and none of the social graces that we would consider necessary for interaction with the rest of the community. So, those kids they didn't know how to, when they left there, they didn't know how to be polite. They had no more idea how to use the setting at a dinner table than the poor kids I had grown up with. They knew it was an alien world that they didn't fit into.

And they adopted a set of beliefs, attitudes and practices which over time prevented them from sort of breaking out. They believed that, you know, the end justified the means. That what I would consider to be ethical and moral behavior was all relative. That everybody was cheating and lying and you were a sucker if you didn't do the same thing. That in the end you had to live hard because chances are you were going to die young. I tell all the folks who I try to help to save money. When I was growing up the older guys always told us only suckers save their money. And if you ran into some money, if you were injured in an accident and you suddenly got a pile of money or you hit the numbers, that the worst thing you could do was save the money and they always had an example of some guy who had come upon some money and he'd saved the money and then he ended up getting hit by a car or being shot or being debilitated and his wife or his kids spent all his money up and what a sucker he was for not spending his money. And this was such a powerful vision that it wasn't until I was much older in life that I realized I had never heard anybody say you should save your money because one day as you get older you're going to need that money. There were no examples of that in our life. So, I'm looking at these beliefs and how solid they were.

He concluded that improving these neighborhoods and the lives that emerged from them required something other than dispensing financial assistance or targeting so-called "categorical" problems of individuals or households, one at a time, as per the social work model. A more effective strategy was to change the sense of what is normal, beginning with small, concrete steps to alter the look and tone of the environment.

Canada began with a single building on 119th Street, a building where drug dealers used vacant units to conduct business, which had the result of driving families out of their apartments even if it meant resorting to homeless shelters. Through a small, preexisting community program, he installed police locks to secure empty units that would otherwise be havens for drug dealers. "We said, Okay, the answer is not social services in this case. The answer is fix the lock on the door."

Next he painted over graffiti on the sides of buildings, and recruited major corporations to send volunteers to clean up parks and vacant lots as a way to influence expectations. Children in particular would get a different visual impression of what an urban neighborhood should look like, and then begin to treat their surroundings accordingly. In this endeavor, Canada astutely played into children's desire to fit in:

If you are nine you come out of your apartment building and there's trash all over the street and you have a soda it would be abnormal for you to walk forty yards to find a trash can to put that can in when you see trash all over everywhere. And kids don't want to be abnormal. They want to be normal. So you come out your building and there is no trash on the street and you have some trash. Well, chances are you're going to go put it in a garbage can. This sense of how do we send these messages to people about what the norm is to me is something that we became really focused on. So, it was cleaning things up. Let's say I'm a parent. I've got three kids and a little one-bedroom apartment who are 8, 9 and 10. I can't go to the park because the park is not useable for young people. That's a tough existence. It wears families out. We went in and we cleaned that whole place up. We painted all the chairs. We just said let's turn this thing back into a park.

He found that the effort to change the norms of one block, then another and another would pay off, as more and more kids responded to visible signs of what is expected:

> I had this social experiment in my mind. We eliminated all the graffiti along a five-block corridor. Then I was going to track how soon it came back. I thought, kids see a fresh thing, first maybe there will be a resistance, but I thought they'd probably come back within three months. That it would come back and we would see kids starting to tag again. See all the graffiti. It never came back. Ever...

The norms of the neighborhood were changing, he realized. More broadly, norms could be actively changed.

These small successes inspired a far more ambitious effort that became the Harlem Children's Zone, touching the lives of more than twenty thousand young people annually. From its small start in 1991, it grew into a $58 million annual enterprise by 2018, depending on private philanthropy for the overwhelming majority of the project revenue. At critical junctures, Canada's dream survived because of major gifts from two billionaire supporters: Stanley Druckenmiller, a hedge fund investor at Duquesne Capital (also a Bowdoin College alumnus), and Kenneth Langone, a cofounder of the Home Depot store chain.

When Canada chose to focus on formative efforts, it was a wrenching decision—as it had likewise been for Brace—since it meant *not* saving young adults who were struggling. Instead, he concentrated his efforts on young children, and on infants and their parents, with the goal of changing the attitudes and life trajectories of those who had not yet abandoned school, fallen into crime, or had a child out of wedlock—the sorts of things that typically qualify one for government-funded intervention. He first offered early education programs, and eventually served elementary and high school students as well, many of them in schools run by the Harlem Children's Zone itself.

To some extent, the Children's Zone became a "cradle-to-college" social program under centralized management, offering some services of the kind that for decades had been provided in publicly funded programs, such as medical and dental clinics. But it is much more, too. Canada aimed to give poor, minority children and adolescents the same sort of "aspirational" environment that nurtures the middle class. The services are necessary but not sufficient to achieve what he had in mind. "I believe in providing high-quality support for kids," he says. "We have good health services here. We have good social services here. But, again, I tell folks to do what middle-class people do. Middle-class people, when their kids need help in algebra they don't send them to play chess. Get them an algebra tutor, right?"

Just as the Henry Street Settlement's homemaking classes prepared young women for married life, the Children's Zone offers a Baby College for new and expectant parents, dispensing information about childhood nutrition and middle-class childrearing methods through a curriculum developed in consultation with a world-famous pediatrician. Corporal punishment should be replaced by timeouts. Encouragement should be more frequent than discouragement. A prekindergarten program, Harlem Gems, emphasizes reading. After-school tutoring helps kids in nearby public schools, and neighborhood kids can choose the ambitious K–12 Promise Academy charter schools, which are supported (like all charters) with a combination of public and private funds, but managed by the Children's Zone. Promise Academy schools are characterized by "long hours and tough rules," with students wearing uniforms and teachers in business attire. The goal is academic success leading to college, whether in the Ivy League or at a New York City community college.

The broader goal is to make academic achievement and college attendance look normal for young people in the neighborhood—as normal as a neighborhood without trash on the street or graffiti on the walls. Kids will get the message that they can do well in school, aim for college, and still fit in with their peers.

> If you are surrounded by people who are always talking about going to college, you're going to end up thinking, "Hey, maybe this is something I could do, too." You can't help but get contaminated by that idea. It just seeps into your pores, and you don't even know that you've caught the virus.

And that kind of contamination can be spread. If we touch enough kids at the same time with the same message, then it won't seem unusual to think, "I should do well in school, I should speak proper English, I should do my homework." These things won't seem like you're not being from the hood or you're not keeping it real. And the same way that this went bad, that it went from kids being respectful and decent to kids being disrespectful and indecent, I think it can go good.[10]

Wilbur Cohen might have approved of these efforts, but they have nothing to do with income support or social workers intervening in already troubled families. Rather, they represent a renaissance of norm setting. The underlying premise is that those touched by the Harlem Children's Zone are not inherently deficient or immoral; they have simply not been exposed to constructive norms. Instead, they have been influenced by dysfunctional norms. Like the newsboys of the nineteenth century, they have had their own norms, but not the kind that lead to a stable, middle-class household—which is the goal that Geoffrey Canada believes they should strive for.

> I want my kids growing up with a sense of orderliness and safety, a belief in what I would call the American Dream—for kids to believe by working hard that the sky's the limit, that they can go as high as their talent will take them. These are, to me, all of the sort of values and attitudes kids need to have to be successful.

Those values, says Canada, help the Children's Zone transcend the need for social service programs.

> We have a much lower teen pregnancy rate than we could by running a pregnancy prevention program. Kids who believe they can go on to college, who really believe that, they are not trying to have a baby.... Most of the kids I know who get pregnant they were like, ah, well yeah I knew, but, you know, I didn't care. And, you know, you don't care because you don't think there is anything better coming....
> Are we trying to inspire our kids to emulate a set of values that we would associate with the middle class? I think the answer to

that is yes. Education is a way, living a clean lifestyle is a way. We don't want them smoking cigarettes, we don't want them drinking, we certainly don't want them using drugs. Some of them do all of that. But the message they get from us is "that's not what we are preparing you for."

This preparation depends not only on academics but also on the modeling of character. For this reason, Canada declines requests to tour the Promise Academy by popular celebrities, especially rap stars prone to celebrating violence and the full range of Union Avenue values. The prospect of financial support from such celebrities does not tempt him.

Although the Promise Academy is not New York's most successful charter school in terms of academic achievement, its results are strongly positive, and the same is true of the other education programs of the Children's Zone.[11] Of the children whose parents enrolled in Baby College, 97 percent (more than 6,000 students) have graduated from high school. Every child enrolled in the Harlem Gems prekindergarten program in 2017 tested as kindergarten-ready. As of 2017, there were 861 graduates of the Promise Academy charter schools attending college. For the 2016–17 school year, eighth-grade students at the Promise Academy II outperformed a "comparison group" of similar students selected by New York City's Department of Education on math proficiency tests (65 percent of the Promise Academy's students were proficient, compared with 54 percent of the comparison group). In English and language arts, 49 percent of the Promise Academy students were proficient, compared with 48 percent of the comparison group. It's worth noting that admission to the school is by lottery, and not all the students have gone through the entire Children's Zone program. At the same time, it's also possible that members of the comparison group were helped (or "contaminated") by HCZ through its after-school tutoring in regular Harlem schools in its 119-block area.

The statistics above are heartening, but Canada's most important report card is a long-term one. He will grade himself not just on how many students go to college, but on how many finish. What matters most is the life trajectory of all the people the Harlem Children's Zone touches, including those who receive extra help after class in New York City public schools. Canada focuses less on convincing gang members to go straight than on depleting their ranks by attrition over time. He cares about the end game for young people who adopt the norms of hard work, savings, and manners; he wants to see them mature to find jobs, to form households, to have children reared by mothers and fathers married to each other.

Moreover, measuring improvements in the 119-block neighborhood is not necessarily the point: neighborhoods change for all sorts of reasons (including a recent influx of affluent residents into Harlem). The Children's Zone is a success if those whose lives it touches improve any neighborhood in which they settle, and if they raise successful children. That's what happens when middle-class norms take hold. The benefits emerge slowly and gradually, as Canada emphasizes:

> We never thought you could do it in a day or two.... We are graduating about a couple hundred kids a year with college degrees and we are just going to keep churning that out over twenty years. That's the only thing that we know that brings intergenerational success. Those kids with degrees, the likelihood is their kids will also go to college, get degrees, pay taxes....
>
> Are they going to form families? Are they going to take care of their families? That to me is an issue that I care about. And everything else can get you distracted, people can take potshots or not, or you can feel excited, that's not what I'm excited about.

Geoffrey Canada is an inspiring "social service" leader who has rediscovered norms as the key to a better life. And his method resonates outside of Harlem. Beginning in 2003, HCZ launched a Practitioners Institute to conduct national and international workshops teaching its "comprehensive, place-based approach to educating children and rebuilding an entire community... struggling with issues like poverty, poor health, failing schools and high crime rates." The Practitioners Institute has "hosted workshops for 477 U.S. communities, from Baltimore to the Cherokee Nation in Oklahoma, and 161 international delegations from countries such as Indonesia, Romania and Singapore." The Children's Zone is forthright in saying that its approach does not provide quick solutions, but does offer promise when there is commitment to the effort: "We tell visitors straight-out: this is tough work and you need to have long-term commitment to see kids all the way to adulthood. There is no quick fix or magic solution—but there is hope."[12]

The history of social services in the United States makes plain that this "tough work" is not best conducted through government agencies or organizations with government contracts. Indeed, a government effort to replicate the Harlem Children's Zone on a larger scale has inadvertently confirmed this fact. In 2010, President Barack Obama's Department of Education tried to scale the HCZ model through what it called "Promise Neighborhoods." By 2015, $100 million in federal grants had been awarded to neighborhoods in twenty states and the District of Columbia, explicitly inspired by HCZ. But no new organizations were being built from scratch, the way Geoffrey Canada personally built the Children's Zone. Instead, a shared data system would knit together a range of existing federally funded social service programs—Head Start, health services, neighborhood schools, and various community groups.

The Education Department described its goal as "Integrating programs and breaking down agency 'silos' so that solutions are implemented effectively and efficiently across agencies."[13] Promise Neighborhood grants were intended to "provide critical support for the planning and implementation of comprehensive services ranging from early learning, K–12, to college and career, including programs to improve the health, safety, and stability of neighborhoods, as well as to boost family engagement in student learning and improve access to learning technology." The department announced in 2012 that another round of grants would "continue to support the creation of plans for providing high-need communities with cradle-to-career services with great schools at the center."[14]

The program was supposed to engineer a "cradle-to-career pipeline" for services, and thereby "to provide equal access and support to disadvantaged children," according to Arne Duncan, the secretary of education.[15] The consulting firm Mathematica echoed that summary of the program's aims: "Promise Neighborhoods seek to offset the effects of growing up in poverty by building a comprehensive continuum of 'cradle-to-career' supports that enable children to reach their potential."[16]

Missing entirely from the federally funded version of the Children's Zone was any mention of middle-class values as a key to that goal. Indeed, Mathematica's evaluation of five representative Promise Neighborhoods in 2015 focused almost entirely on bureaucratic "benchmarks," noting, for instance, that "the five case study sites have established networks of partners collaborating in new and different ways." What's more, "leaders of different organizations get to know each other and build trust based on a commitment to the common agenda."[17] The best the Mathematica evaluation could say about the impact of Promise Neighborhoods was that "all sites reported upward trends in some measures and downward trends in others."[18]

The government effort to spread Geoffrey Canada's vision nationwide was complicated, as well, by a basic fact of the public sector: elections lead to policy change. The Trump administration recommended reducing the annual budget for the national program from $73 million to $60 million—roughly the one-year budget for the Harlem Children's Zone alone. A visionary who builds an organization on personal commitment and purpose—such as Charles Loring Brace, or Jane Addams, or Lillian Wald, or Geoffrey Canada—is unlikely to change course with the political winds.

Nor would increased funding translate into effectiveness. More money could not overcome what Nathan Glazer called the limits of social policy: what government can effectively influence and what is beyond its reach.[19] And as the Promise Neighborhoods initiative suggests, government may not understand the nature of the problem.

While Geoffrey Canada stands out for his faith in middle-class values as a means to improve the lives of the poor and their children, others have independently been inspired to infuse middle-class values into poor neighborhoods. One of these is Alice Ely Chapman, who inherited a Connecticut newspaper fortune after a modest career as an administrator in a Philadelphia private school. In 1999, she purchased and renovated an abandoned school building in Marietta, Ohio, and set up a tutoring and recreation program to serve the area's poor white Appalachian population, in which many parents have succumbed to drug use. Her building also hosts the local Boy Scout troop. The Ely Chapman Education Foundation has reached two thousand kids in a city whose population totals fifteen thousand. Chapman's goals are to encourage independent learning, good study habits, and the work ethic. To illustrate her teaching of personal responsibility, she recounts a situation in which a student says the teacher forgot to distribute the day's homework assignment, which students are to bring with them to the ECEF session. Chapman says that completing the assignment is still the responsibility of the student, who knows that homework is routine and should therefore have sought it out.[20]

When Mack McCarter, a minister from the Disciples of Christ mainline Protestant denomination, founded the Community Renewal initiative in Shreveport, Louisiana, in 1994, he borrowed explicitly from the early Hull House model. His "Friendship Houses" bring young married couples to live in Shreveport's poor black Allandale section—a classic other-side-of-the tracks neighborhood where "shotgun houses" sit next to ditch-style sewers. A Friendship House is like "a community center in a home," McCarter explains. It is "a place for after-school education programs, character building, service projects, GED courses, tutoring, computer training, art and music lessons, family nights, and much more." Those who live in a Friendship House with their families are called "Community Coordinators," and they offer guidance and a model of middle-class values, along with youth clubs and adult literacy classes. They serve as "catalysts for rebuilding safe and caring neighborhoods," says McCarter. "They spend time with the neighbors, earning their trust. The relationships they form become a foundation for residents to set and achieve basic goals in the areas of community, education, leadership, housing, health, safety, and meaningful work."

There are obvious differences between these three independent idealists—a black former community organizer, a middle-aged Yankee heiress, and a southern white minister. Yet they all hit upon a norms-focused model for turning a poor neighborhood into one that is safe, and for encouraging self-improvement and personal aspiration. If there is hope for middle-class values taking hold in places where they have been attenuated, this is how it will happen—not through yet another government-led initiative.

# REFLECTIONS ON
# SOCIAL NORMS

W hile these chapters have focused on the importance of spreading bourgeois norms to poor neighborhoods, it would be a mistake to infer that those norms are fully operative in most relatively well-off American households—or, for that matter, in affluent households in other developed countries. Longstanding values pertaining to courtship, marriage, manners, self-restraint, deferred gratification, and religious observance have been eroding across the culture.

The weakening of these values is reflected in a wide range of indicators, from the character of public discourse to the decline of groups such as the Boy Scouts, whose membership fell from 3.35 million in 2000 to just 2.5 million in 2013.[1] The skyrocketing and debilitating use of opioids, across social classes, represents a dispirited retreat from the belief in fulfillment through work and steady self-improvement—an understanding of the difference between satisfaction and passing pleasure. Therefore, I am not arguing that poor minority groups and immigrants are the only segments of the population remote from the "aspirational culture" of which Geoffrey Canada speaks.

Nor do I assert, as some would, that the welfare state's income transfer payments are responsible for eroding bourgeois norms. Certainly the structure of such benefits—whether for health care, housing, or general assistance—may reduce incentives to work, as when a household's rent in the public housing system is based on a percentage of its earned income, or when a household's increased earnings would jeopardize its eligibility for subsidized health insurance (as the economist Casey Mulligan has argued).[2] But it is hard to dispute the view that some forms of public relief are appropriate and necessary. Poverty can be the result of sheer insufficiency and insecurity today, just as Robert Hunter believed in 1904.[3] I do not propose a massive rollback of the welfare state, nor do I endorse the view of nineteenth-century figures such as Josephine Shaw Lowell that idleness among the poor (as well as among the rich!) is the result of a character defect.[4] The prospects for employment depend, to some extent, on markets beyond the control of individuals.

Still, it is possible to be raised in a deleterious environment, a home where one is not exposed to the bourgeois norms that provide a foundation for individual and societal prosperity. The economic historian Deirdre McCloskey makes the case that ethical behavior is closely linked to the success of a free-market economy, contrary to what the critics of capitalism assert. Her masterpiece, *Bourgeois Virtues*, presents a historical view of the "ethical soil in which an economy grows."[5] My own variation on McCloskey's theme is that bourgeois norms—from education to temperance and so much more—are the ethical soil in which individuals and their communities can thrive. This was self-evident to nineteenth-century moral reformers, but it was forgotten in the twentieth-century campaigns to ensure at least a minimum of income security for all amid the vicissitudes of the modern economy.

Charles Loring Brace understood that gambling was not going to help newsboys husband their meager income. Jane Addams understood that immigrants would have limited chances for upward mobility unless they made the effort to learn the language of their new country—one aspect of adopting its norms. Geoffrey Canada understands that when some modicum of income security is virtually assured for all American households (thanks to Wilbur Cohen and his heirs), what truly puts poor children at a disadvantage is the absence of a structured and stimulating home life.

Bringing bourgeois norms into poor neighborhoods was the goal of the settlement houses, and it is the goal of the Harlem Children's Zone. The revival of this principle, as Joel Schwartz argues in *Fighting Poverty with Virtue*, offers a way of resolving "a rigidly polarized debate between left and right about poverty." Promoting bourgeois virtues does not amount to "blaming the victim," but rather it provides "a route out of victimhood."[6] There is no guarantee that even the best habits—"thrift, industry, and sobriety," as Schwartz summarizes them—will ensure economic prosperity or even security. But absent those virtues, one's chances of establishing and maintaining a middle-class household, and enjoying the satisfactions associated with it, are nil.

It may well be true that the existence of income transfer and redistribution programs offered by government can lure the poor into dependency. Josephine Shaw Lowell made that argument in the nineteenth century, and Charles Murray in the twentieth. There is no doubt that specific incentives in public assistance programs—such as the time limits and work requirements that were incorporated into federal public assistance law in 1996—can modify the behavior of recipients. But history makes clear that while government can provide financial assistance or basic shelter, and can set the terms for such provision, it is not the right instrument for instilling the bourgeois norms that are central to a culture of aspiration. It remains incumbent on the institutions of civil society to present a vision of the greater material comfort and life satisfaction that come from a life of thrift, sobriety, savings, education, ambition, and work.

Efforts from civil society to do exactly that are pushing against powerful tides today. In earlier times, elites believed in bourgeois norms, and were willing and eager to defend them. Elite opinion has changed.

In *The Contradictions of Capitalism* (1976), the sociologist Daniel Bell traced a decline in the defense of bourgeois norms following the vast increase of wealth engendered by capitalism. Ironically, this wealth seeded attitudes contrary to those that had fueled the success of capitalism. Bell—himself the son of Lower East Side New York garment workers, such as those who might have gone to the Henry Street Settlement—identified a "distinctive culture and character structure" that were connected with a capitalist mode of economic operation:

In culture, this was the idea of self-realization, the release of the individual from traditional ascriptive ties (family and birth) so that he could "make" of himself what he willed. In character structure, this was the norm of self-control and delayed gratification, of purposeful behavior in the pursuit of well-defined goals. It is the interrelationship of this economic system, culture and character structure, which comprised bourgeois civilization.[7]

Another key to the success of emerging capitalism was a union of "asceticism and acquisitiveness," or to put it another way, a combination of the "bourgeois prudential spirit of calculation" with a "restless Faustian drive." In Bell's analysis, "The intertwining of the two impulses shaped the modern conception of rationality. The tension between the two imposed a moral restraint on the sumptuary display that had characterized earlier periods of conquest."[8]

The prosperity of the twentieth century, however, led to the "unraveling of that unity" of the purposeful and the ascetic life. With wealth came Modernism, emphasizing creativity, self-expression, and unlimited experience. Modernism was "the agency for the dissolution of the bourgeois world view," according to Bell. "Modernism has been a rage against order and, specifically, against bourgeois orderliness." Most crucially, it brought the insistence "that experience is to have no boundaries on its cravings, that there be 'nothing sacred.'"[9]

Writers after Bell, on the other hand, have observed that while the affluent may be reluctant to use such terms as "middle-class values," and even more so to preach their benefits, that doesn't mean they don't live by such values. David Brooks coined the label "bourgeois bohemian" for those who combine the expression of Modernist attitudes with the practice of bourgeois behavior in their own lives. Others have observed that the reluctance to endorse bourgeois values openly has had especially ill effects on the poor, who become entrapped in a culture of dependency and financial limitation as the welfare state expands. Charles Murray has posited that some of the poor remain poor simply because they lack the motivation to go to work in the morning.

Myron Magnet, former editor of *City Journal*, the Manhattan Institute's quarterly, linked the emergence of a permanently poor "underclass" mired in poverty and antisocial behavior to a failure of the "majority culture" to endorse bourgeois values. In his landmark book, *The Dream and the Nightmare*, he wrote that "American culture underwent a revolution in the 1960s, which transformed some of its most basic beliefs and values," and that "many of the new culture's beliefs downplayed the personal responsibility, self-control, and deferral of gratification that it takes to succeed." Magnet concluded, "When these new attitudes reached the poor, particularly the urban, minority poor, the result was catastrophic."[10]

Kay Hymowitz, our colleague at the Manhattan Institute, has built upon Magnet's insight, noting that the affluent have continued to live their own lives based on bourgeois values, and the result is an increasing divergence between the lives and prospects of the rich and the poor. In *Marriage and Caste in America*, Hymowitz linked the likelihood of intergenerational poverty with the failure of poor households to follow what she called a "life script" based on education, raising children within marriage, and providing the sort of mental stimulation that Geoffrey Canada has sought to encourage at his Baby College—what she calls the parents' mission.[11]

Daniel Bell saw an inevitable push in democracies to reduce income inequality by political means—as apt an observation today as it was in the 1970s. Income redistribution programs, including health insurance for the poor (Medicaid) and a wide range of cash assistance, are clearly a permanent fixture of the political system, though the terms of receipt may vary. (In 2018, for instance, the Trump administration proposed a work requirement for those receiving Medicaid.) Latter-day acolytes of Josephine Shaw Lowell who might believe that drastic cuts in transfer payments are the surest way to motivate a culture of aspiration—through desperation—are likely to be disappointed. The question, then, is whether a successful promotion of bourgeois norms aimed at creating a culture of aspiration among the poor can coexist with the welfare state.

The first step toward reviving a culture of aspiration is to acknowledge that norms matter, and that changing them calls for serious effort from outside the agencies of government. Americans have become accustomed to new "programs" as a response to social problems, so it runs against the political grain to assert that no new government program can do the job. A renewal of bourgeois norms will require decentralized action and personal commitment—such as Stanley Druckenmiller's dedication of much of his personal fortune to the Harlem Children's Zone. Or Alice Chapman's decision to create something similar in southern Ohio. Or Geoffrey Canada's personal decision to steer clear of rap music stars who offer to tour the Children's Zone. In short, it requires a renaissance of civil society.

What would such a renaissance mean for the multibillion-dollar social service state? It cannot easily be reined in or rolled back. Each program mounted by entities such as the Administration for Children and Families not only has a politically popular agenda—improving nutrition, combating drug abuse, promoting early education—it also has a constituency of employees. Shuttering these agencies, or even reducing their budgets, would result in political firestorms. Can the staff of such agencies at least be trained and encouraged to do no harm? That would entail returning social work to its roots of friendly visiting: exposing households to the idea that life choices can improve life chances, rather than compensating them with services for being victims of an unjust social structure.

In the longer run, one can hope for the visions of people like Geoffrey Canada, Alice Chapman, and Mack McCarter to take hold more widely. If a moral rearmament occurs, the perceived need for social services could diminish. Wilbur Cohen hoped that an income safety net would free those receiving help to work and strive, such that ultimately they would not need financial help. But that, of course, did not prove to be a justified faith.

Nor can one be pollyana-ish about full employment for all the willing and able. The rapid pace of technological change means that even those who are skilled, disciplined, and motivated can face disruption—and unemployment. Nonetheless, the wisdom of Jane Addams has enduring pertinence: "Working people...require only that their aspirations be recognized and stimulated, and the means of attaining them put at their disposal."[12]

The twin ideas of personal encouragement and individual responsibility, and the message that the social and economic systems in America will welcome those who are prepared to take advantage of opportunity, add up to an optimistic vision for the future, but a vision that is supported by history. It merits rediscovery and renewal.

# ACKNOWLEDGMENTS

My thanks to Nick Ohnell, the Achelis & Bodman Foundation, and the John Templeton Foundation for their generous support. Thanks, as well, to my Manhattan Institute colleagues, and particularly Lawrence Mone, president; Vanessa Mendoza, executive vice president; Brian Anderson, editor of *City Journal*, and his predecessor, Myron Magnet; and Bernadette Serton, book program director. All provided invaluable editorial suggestions. For their counsel and time, I am grateful to Geoffrey Canada, Richard Gelles, and Dan Scheneider. My deep appreciation also to my first great editor, William Miller of the former *Boston Phoenix*, and to Helen Gregutt, my high school English teacher at South Euclid Lyndhurst public schools in Ohio. Finally, thanks to *City Journal* and the *Wilson Quarterly* for publishing earlier versions of portions of this book.

# NOTES

## INTRODUCTION—HOW CIVIL SOCIETY SAVED MY FATHER

1 Juvenile Aid Society meeting minutes, Philadelphia, March 22, 1934; Association for Jewish Children (Philadelphia) Records, 1855–1973, Special Collections Research Center, Temple University Libraries, Philadelphia.

2 Association for Jewish Children archives, Balch Institute for Ethnic Studies, Philadelphia.

3 Ibid.

4 Ron Haskins, "Three Simple Rules Poor Teens Should Follow to Join the Middle Class," Brookings Institution, March 2013.

5 Mary Parke, "Are Married Parents Really Better for Children? What Research Shows about the Effect of Family Structure on Child Well-Being," Center for Law and Social Policy, May 2003.

6 Wendy Wang and W. Bradford Wilcox, "The Millennial Success Sequence: Marriage, Kids, and the 'Success Sequence' among Young Adults," AEI and Institute for Family Studies, June 14, 2017. Quotation from the AEI "Summary of Key Points."

7 Richard Gelles, "Creating an Effective Child Welfare System," in *Urban Policy Frontiers* (Manhattan Institute for Policy Research, 2017), p. 59.

8 National Institute on Drug Abuse, Overdose Death Rates, August 2018, https://www.drugabuse.gov/related-topics/trends-statistics/overdose-death-rates

9 Edward L. Glaeser, "The War on Work—and How to End It," *City Journal: The Shape of Work to Come*, Special Issue, 2017, https://www.city-journal.org/html/war-work-and-how-end-it-15250.html

10 See Scott Winship, "Economic Mobility: A State of the Art Primer," Archbridge Institute, March 2017. Winship finds that 64 percent of thirty-year-olds in 2010, 2011, and 2012 had higher inflation-adjusted incomes, including federal cash transfers, than their parents at the same age, but in 1970 the figure was 70 percent.

11 Charles Murray, *Coming Apart: The State of White America, 1960–2010* (New York: Crown Forum, 2012), p. 309.

12 Robert Putnam, *Our Kids: The American Dream in Crisis* (New York: Simon & Schuster, 2015), p. 41.

13 Charles Loring Brace, "Saving and Gambling," *Short Sermons to News Boys: With a History of the Formation of the News Boys' Lodging-House* (New York: Charles Scribner & Co., 1866), pp. 162–63.

14 Jane Addams, *Twenty Years at Hull-House, with Autobiographical Notes* (1910; Urbana: University of Illinois Press, 1990), p. 136.

15  Elizabeth T. Agnew, *From Charity to Social Work: Mary E. Richmond and the Creation of an American Profession* (Urbana: University of Illinois Press, 2004), p. 164.

16  Lesley Brody, "Ian Rowe: A Class on Life Knowledge," *Wall Street Journal*, March 12, 2018.

17  Joel Schwartz, *Fighting Poverty with Virtue: Moral Reform and America's Urban Poor, 1825–2000* (Bloomington: Indiana University Press, 2000), p. xviii.

18  Sarah L. Pettijohn and Elizabeth T. Boris et al., "Nonprofit-Government Contracts and Grants: Findings from the 2013 National Survey," Urban Institute, December 2013, p. 1.

19  Nathan Glazer, *The Limits of Social Policy* (Cambridge, Mass.: Harvard University Press, 1988), p. 7.

20  Agnew, *From Charity to Social Work*, p. 165.

21  "Council on Social Work Education Core Competencies: Diversity in Practice," in Mark J. Stern and June Axinn, *Social Welfare: A History of the American Response to Need*, 8th ed. (New York: Pearson, 2012), Exhibit (unnumbered page).

22  Ibid.

23  Michael Powell, "In Fighting Teen Pregnancy, the Folly of Shame and Blame," *New York Times*, March 11, 2013.

24  See, for example, Georgia Center for Opportunity, "The Success Sequence," YouTube, December 4, 2018, https://www.youtube.com/watch?v=PCUp4fkfgV8

25  James Q. Wilson, *The Marriage Problem: How Our Culture Has Weakened Families* (New York: HarperCollins, 2002), p. 221.

26  Geoffrey Canada, *Reaching Up for Manhood* (Boston: Beacon Press, 1998), p. 121.

27  Of the 1,491 students who have taken part in some program at the Ely Chapman Education Foundation since 1999, 88 percent have gone on to graduate from high school, compared with 82 percent citywide—despite the fact that only 17 percent of those students live with their two biological parents and more than half are from low-income households.

CHAPTER 1 — CHARLES LORING BRACE:
"TO AVERT RATHER THAN CURE"

1  Robert Bremner, *From the Depths: The Discovery of Poverty in the United States* (Washington Square: New York University Press, 1956), p. xi.

2  Ibid., p. 47.

3  Ibid., p. 33.

4  Ibid., pp. 36–37.

5  Emma Brace, *The Life of Charles Loring Brace, Chiefly Told in His Own Letters*, edited by his daughter (New York: Charles Scribner's Sons, 1894), p. 5.

6  Charles Loring Brace, *Address to the Theological Students of Harvard University: On the Methods and Aims of a Charity for the Children of the Poor, May 12th, 1881* (Cambridge, Mass.: Harvard Divinity School, 1881).

7  Ibid.

8  Ibid.

9 Emma Brace, *The Life of Charles Loring Brace*, p. 57.

10 Ibid., p. 117.

11 Ibid., p. 54.

12 Ibid., p. 154.

13 Ibid., p. 156.

14 Ibid., p. 154.

15 Brace, *Address to the Theological Students*.

16 Bremner, *From the Depths*, pp. 212–13.

17 Jay Shambaugh, Lauren Bauer, and Audrey Breitwieser, "Who Is Poor in the United States? A Hamilton Project Annual Report," Brookings, October 12, 2017.

18 Horatio Alger, *Ragged Dick; Or, Street Life in New York With the Boot-Blacks* (Philadelphia: John C. Winston Co., 1868), p. 3.

19 Brace, *Address to the Theological Students*.

20 Ibid.

21 Frances Fox Piven and Richard Cloward, *Regulating the Poor: The Functions of Public Welfare* (New York: Pantheon Books, 1971).

22 Charles Loring Brace, *The Dangerous Classes of New York, and Twenty Years' Work Among Them* (New York: Wynkoop & Hallenbeck, 1872), p. 347.

23 Brace, *Address to the Theological Students*, p. 6.

24 Brace, *The Dangerous Classes of New York*, pp. 80–81.

25 Brace, "Saving and Gambling," *Short Sermons to News Boys: With a History of the Formation of the News Boys' Lodging-House* (New York: Charles Scribner & Co., 1866), pp. 155–65.

26 Brace, *The Dangerous Classes of New York*, p. 225.

27 Ibid.

28 Mark J. Stern and June Axinn, *Social Welfare: A History of the American Response to Need*, 8th ed. (New York: Pearson, 2012), p. 56.

29 Emma Brace, *The Life of Charles Loring Brace*, Appendix C.

30 Stern and Axinn, *Social Welfare*, p. 58.

31 Brace, *The Dangerous Classes of New York*, p. 18.

32 Brace, *Address to the Theological Students*, p. 10.

33 Ibid., pp. 17–18.

34 Ibid., p. 21.

35 Emma Brace, *The Life of Charles Loring Brace*, p. 253.

36 Ibid., p. 306.

37 Brace, *Address to the Theological Students*, p. 20.

38 Ibid., p. 24.

39 Ibid.

40 Brace, *The Dangerous Classes of New York*, p. 284.

41 Ibid., pp. 284–85.

42 Children's Aid Society, New York, Consolidated Financial Statements (Together with Independent Auditors' Report) for the Years Ended June 30, 2016 and 2015.

43 Brace, *Address to the Theological Students*, p. 21.

44 Brace, *The Dangerous Classes of New York*, p. 198.

45 Ibid., p. 234.

46 Ibid., p. 244.

47  Ibid., pp. 265–66.
48  Andrew Polsky, *The Rise of the Therapeutic State* (Princeton, N.J.: Princeton University Press, 1991), p. 12.
49  Brace, *Address to the Theological Students*, p. 18.
50  *Eighth Annual Report of the Children's Aid Society*, February, 1861 (New York: Wynkoop, Hallenbeck & Thomas, 1861), p. 37, reprinted in *Annual Reports of the Children's Aid Society*, Nos. 1–10, Feb. 1854 – Feb. 1863 (New York: Arno Press and The New York Times, 1971).
51  *Seventh Annual Report of the Children's Aid Society*, February, 1860 (New York: Wynkoop, Hallenbeck & Thomas, 1860), p. 62, reprinted in *Annual Reports of the Children's Aid Society*, Nos. 1–10.
52  Ibid., p. 63.
53  Brace, *The Dangerous Classes of New York*, p. 269.
54  Emma Brace, *The Life of Charles Loring Brace*, p. 481.
55  Ibid.

CHAPTER 2—JANE ADDAMS: FROM NORMS TO REFORM

1  James Weber Linn, *Jane Addams: A Biography* (Urbana: University of Illinois Press, 2000), p. 11.
2  Jane Addams, *Twenty Years at Hull-House, with Autobiographical Notes* (1910; Urbana: University of Illinois Press, 1990), pp. 4–5.
3  Ibid., p. 9.
4  Ibid., p. 122.
5  Jane Addams, "The Function of the Social Settlement," American Academy of Political and Social Science, Philadelphia, 1899.
6  Addams, *Twenty Years at Hull-House*, p. 4.
7  Ibid., p. 150.
8  Ibid., p. 154.
9  Ibid., p. 123.
10 Ibid.
11 Robert A. Woods and Albert J. Kennedy, eds., *Handbook of Settlements* (New York: Russell Sage Foundation, 1913).
12 Charles Loring Brace, "Child Saving as Shown in Summer Homes and Sanitaria near Large Cities," National Conference of Charities and Correction, St. Louis, October 15, 1884.
13 Linn, *Jane Addams: A Biography*, p. 154.
14 Woods and Kennedy, *Handbook of Settlements*, pp. 283–84.
15 Lillian D. Wald, *The House on Henry Street* (New York: Henry Holt & Co., 1915), p. 98.
16 Ibid., p. 108.
17 Locust Street Settlement House, Social Welfare History Project, VCU Libraries, https://socialwelfare.library.vcu.edu/settlement-houses/locust-street/
18 *Negro Year Book: An Annual Encyclopedia of the Negro, 1918–1919*, ed. Monroe N. Work (Tuskegee Institute, Alabama: Negro Year Book Publishing Co., 1919).
19 Jacqueline Anne Rouse, *Lugenia Burns Hope: Black Southern Reformer* (Athens, Ga.: University of Georgia Press, 1989), p. 70.
20 Ibid., p. 89.

21 Ibid., p. 90.
22 Ibid., p. 7.
23 Ibid., p. 71.
24 Linn, *Jane Addams: A Biography*, p. 115.
25 Ibid., p. 111.
26 Ibid., p. 129.
27 Lela B. Costin, *Two Sisters for Social Justice: A Biography of Grace and Edith Abbott* (Urbana: University of Illinois Press, 1983), p. 46.
28 Michael B. Katz, *In the Shadow of the Poorhouse: A Social History of Welfare in America* (New York: Basic Books, 1986), p. 126.
29 Costin, *Two Sisters for Social Justice*, p. 48.
30 Linn, *Jane Addams: A Biography*, p. 284.
31 Katz, *In the Shadow of the Poorhouse*, p. 123.
32 Joel Schwartz, *Fighting Poverty with Virtue: Moral Reform and America's Urban Poor, 1825–2000* (Bloomington: Indiana University Press, 2000), p. 112.
33 Ibid., p. 113.
34 Charles Murray, "Belmont & Fishtown," *New Criterion*, January 2012.

CHAPTER 3—MARY RICHMOND:
FROM "SCIENTIFIC CHARITY" TO SOCIAL WORK

1 Robert Bremner, *From the Depths: The Discovery of Poverty in the United States* (Washington Square: New York University Press, 1956), p. 50.
2 Josephine Shaw Lowell, *Public Relief and Private Charity* (New York: G. P. Putnam's Sons, Knickerbocker Press, 1884), p. 259.
3 Bremner, *From the Depths*, p. 51
4 Ibid., p. 52.
5 Michael B. Katz, *In the Shadow of the Poorhouse: A Social History of Welfare in America* (New York: Basic Books, 1986), pp. 77–78.
6 Ibid., p. 83.
7 Elizabeth T. Agnew, *From Charity to Social Work: Mary E. Richmond and the Creation of an American Profession* (Urbana: University of Illinois Press, 2004), pp. 19–20.
8 Ibid., p. 25.
9 Ibid., p. 29.
10 Ibid., p. 32.
11 Ibid., p. 55.
12 Ibid., pp. 65–66, 71–72.
13 Ibid., p. 138.
14 Robert Hunter, *Poverty* (New York: Macmillan, 1904), p. 4.
15 Ibid., pp. 3–4.
16 Agnew, *From Charity to Social Work*, p. 80, citing speech at a Working Women's Clubs convention.
17 Ibid., p. 73.
18 Mary E. Richmond, *Friendly Visiting Among the Poor: A Handbook for Charity Workers* (New York: Macmillan, 1899), p. 8.
19 Ibid., p. 86.
20 Ibid., pp. 44–45, 78–79, 87, e.g.
21 Ibid., p. 89.

22  Agnew, *From Charity to Social Work*, p. 81.

23  Ibid., p. 82.

24  Mary Ellen Richmond, *Social Diagnosis* (New York: Russell Sage Foundation, 1917), p. 26.

25  Ibid., p. 43.

26  Agnew, *From Charity to Social Work*, p. 158.

27  Charles Richmond Henderson, Foreword to Amelia Sears, *The Charity Visitor: A Handbook for Beginners* (Chicago School of Civics and Philanthropy, 1913).

28  Andrew J. Polsky, *The Rise of the Therapeutic State* (Princeton, N.J.: Princeton University Press, 1991), pp. 112–13.

29  Abraham Flexner, "Is Social Work a Profession?" Address to the 42nd Annual Session of the National Conference of Charities and Correction, Baltimore, May 17, 1915.

30  Agnew, *From Charity to Social Work*, p. 168.

31  Ibid., p. 167.

32  Mary Richmond, "The Social Worker's Task," Presentation at the 44th Meeting of the National Conference on Social Welfare, Pittsburgh, June 6–13, 1917.

33  Agnew, *From Charity to Social Work*, pp. 163–64.

34  Richmond, *Friendly Visiting Among the Poor*, pp. 6–7.

35  Richmond, *Social Diagnosis*, p. 25.

36  Agnew, *From Charity to Social Work*, p. 89.

37  Richmond, *Friendly Visiting Among the Poor*, pp. 7–8.

38  Ibid., pp. 8–9.

39  Agnew, *From Charity to Social Work*, p. 123.

40  Ibid., p. 121.

41  Ibid., p. 123.

42  Polsky, *The Rise of the Therapeutic State*, p. 116.

43  Ibid., p. 20.

44  Ibid., pp. 12–13.

45  Steven Rathgeb Smith and Michael Lipsky, *Nonprofits for Hire: The Welfare State in the Age of Contracting* (Cambridge, Mass.: Harvard University Press, 1993).

46  For example, see the Family and Youth Services Bureau Fact Sheet, Administration for Children and Families, 2017, https://www.acf.hhs.gov/sites/default/files/fysb/2017factsheets_fysb_tempo.pdf

47  Polsky, *The Rise of the Therapeutic State*, pp. 11–12.

48  Amber Daniels, "A Neighborhood Youth Center," in *Days in the Lives of Social Workers: 58 Professionals Tell "Real-Life" Stories from Social Work Practice*, ed. Linda May Grobman, 4th ed. (Harrisburg, Penn.: White Hat Communications, 2012), p. 122.

49  Ibid.

50  Polsky, *The Rise of the Therapeutic State*, p. 18.

## CHAPTER 4 – GRACE ABBOTT FROM NEBRASKA:
### SERVICES RATHER THAN NORMS

1  O. A. Abbott, *Recollections of a Pioneer Lawyer*, ed. Addison E. Sheldon (Lincoln: Nebraska State Historical Society, 1929), p. 5.

2  Ibid., p. 26.
3  Ibid., p. 142.
4  Lela B. Costin, *Two Sisters for Social Justice: A Biography of Grace and Edith Abbott* (Urbana: University of Illinois Press, 1983), p. 10.
5  Ibid., p. 6.
6  Ibid., p. 11.
7  Ibid., pp. 17–18.
8  John Sorensen, Introduction to *The Grace Abbott Reader*, ed. John Sorensen with Judith Sealander (Lincoln: University of Nebraska Press, 2008), p. xi.
9  Grace Abbott, "The Education of Foreigners in American Citizenship," in *The Grace Abbott Reader*, p. 15.
10  Ibid., p. 9.
11  Ibid., pp. 15–16.
12  Costin, *Two Sisters for Social Justice*, p. 71.
13  Ibid., p. 122.
14  Ibid., p. 126.
15  See Blanche D. Coll, *Safety Net: Welfare and Social Security, 1929–1979* (New Brunswick, N.J.: Rutgers University Press, 1995).
16  Clarke A. Chambers, *Seedtime of Reform: American Social Service and Social Action 1918–1933* (Minneapolis: University of Minnesota Press, 1963).
17  I. M. Rubinow, *Social Insurance: With Special Reference to American Conditions* (New York: H. Holt, 1913).
18  Coll, *Safety Net: Welfare and Social Security*, p. 50.
19  Costin, *Two Sisters for Social Justice*, pp. 125–26.
20  Jeanne C. Marsh, Postscript to *The Grace Abbott Reader*, p. 106.
21  Costin, *Two Sisters for Social Justice*, p. 133.
22  Ibid., p. 167.
23  Ibid., p. 166.
24  Ray Lyman Wilbur, Address to the White House Conference on Child Health and Protection, Washington, D.C., November 19–22, 1930 (New York: Century Co., 1931).
25  Ibid.
26  Costin, *Two Sisters for Social Justice*, p. 170.
27  President Herbert Hoover, Opening Address to the White House Conference on Child Health and Protection.
28  Ibid.
29  Costin, *Two Sisters for Social Justice*, pp. 172–73.
30  Sorensen, Introduction to *The Grace Abbott Reader*, p. xiv.
31  Eleanor Roosevelt, "My Day: November 19, 1937," *The Eleanor Roosevelt Papers Digital Edition* (2017), https://www2.gwu.edu/~erpapers/myday/displaydoc.cfm?_y=1937&_f=md054803
32  Sorensen, Introduction to *The Grace Abbott Reader*, p. xiii.
33  Ibid., p. x.
34  Ibid., p. xiii.
35  Coll, *Safety Net: Welfare and Social Security*, p. 39.
36  Ibid., p. 102.
37  An Urban Institute analysis of the "kids' share" of the federal budget estimates that spending on child-related programs of all kinds will total $4.4 trillion in the ten-year period from 2019 through 2028 (if proposed budget

cuts are not adopted). Cary Lou, Julia B. Isaacs, and Ashley Hong, "How Would the President's Proposed 2019 Budget Affect Spending on Children?" Urban Institute, July 2018, Table 1, p. 5.

38  Costin, *Two Sisters for Social Justice*, pp. 228–29.

39  Andrew J. Polsky, *The Rise of the Therapeutic State* (Princeton, N.J.: Princeton University Press, 1991).

40  Coll, *Safety Net: Welfare and Social Security*, p. 60.

41  Lester Salamon, "Of Market Failure, Voluntary Failure, and Third-Party Government: Toward a Theory of Government-Nonprofit Relations in the Modern Welfare State, *Nonprofit and Voluntary Sector Quarterly*, January 1, 1987.

42  Mary E. Richmond, *Friendly Visiting Among the Poor: A Handbook for Charity Workers* (New York: Macmillan, 1899), p. 9.

43  Costin, *Two Sisters for Social Justice*, p. 191.

44  Ibid., p. 19.

45  Ibid., p. 190.

46  Ibid., p. 193.

47  Richmond, *Friendly Visiting Among the Poor*, p. 195.

48  Ibid., p. 181.

49  "Settlement House Dedicated in Bronx: Henry Morgenthau and Wife, Founders of Institution, Attend Ceremony," *New York Times*, March 4, 1929.

50  Costin, *Two Sisters for Social Justice*, p. 230.

51  Ibid., p. 235.

52  Grace Abbott, "Promoting the Welfare of All Children," Speech at the Children's Bureau Dinner, Washington, D.C., April 8, 1937, in *The Grace Abbott Reader*, p. 75.

## CHAPTER 5 — WILBUR COHEN AND THE
## SCALING OF THE SOCIAL SERVICE STATE

1  Edward D. Berkowitz, *Mr. Social Security: The Life of Wilbur J. Cohen* (Lawrence, Kans.: University Press of Kansas, 1995), p. 42.

2  Ibid.

3  Ibid., pp. 7–8.

4  Ibid., p. 11.

5  Ibid., p. 14.

6  Ibid., pp. 13–14.

7  Ibid., pp. 53–54.

8  Blanche D. Coll, *Safety Net: Welfare and Social Security, 1929–1979* (New Brunswick, N.J.: Rutgers University Press, 1995), p. 127.

9  Ibid., p. 128.

10  Ibid., pp. 137–39.

11  Berkowitz, *Mr. Social Security*, p. 94.

12  Ibid., p. 113.

13  Ibid., p. 11.

14  Coll, *Safety Net: Welfare and Social Security*, p. 178.

15  Berkowitz, *Mr. Social Security*, p. 53.

16  Coll, *Safety Net: Welfare and Social Security*, p. 210.

17  Ibid., p. 218.

18  Berkowitz, *Mr. Social Security*, p. 150.

19  Wilbur J. Cohen and Robert M. Ball, "Public Welfare Amendments of 1962 and Proposals for Health Insurance for the Aged," *Social Security Bulletin*, October 1962, pp. 3–16.
20  Berkowitz, *Mr. Social Security*, p. 145.
21  Ibid., p. 224.
22  Mark J. Stern and June Axinn, *Social Welfare: A History of the American Response to Need*, 8th ed. (New York: Pearson, 2012), p. 226.
23  Ibid., p. 237.
24  Ibid., p. 239.
25  Coll, *Safety Net: Welfare and Social Security*, p. 237.
26  Department of Health and Human Services, Office of the Assistant Secretary for Planning and Evaluation, "Trends in AFDC and Food Stamp Benefits, 1972–1994," May 1, 1995.
27  Berkowitz, *Mr. Social Security*, p. 153.
28  Stern and Axinn, *Social Welfare*, p. 239.
29  Administration for Children and Families, Office of Child Care, "Fiscal Year 2018 Federal Child Care and Related Appropriations," May 30, 2018.
30  Martha Derthick, *Uncontrollable Spending for Social Services Grants* (Washington, D.C.: Brookings Institution Press, 1975), p. 3.
31  Ibid.
32  Andrew J. Polsky, *The Rise of the Therapeutic State* (Princeton, N.J.: Princeton University Press, 1991), p. 164.
33  Ibid., p. 185.
34  Ibid., p. 166.
35  Steven Rathgeb Smith and Michael Lipsky, *Nonprofits for Hire: The Welfare State in the Age of Contracting* (Cambridge, Mass.: Harvard University Press, 1993), p. 110.
36  Ibid., p. 113.
37  Ibid., p. 216, citing Martin Bulmer, *The Social Basis for Community Care* (1987).
38  "Drunkenness" and "liquor laws" are given in the *Statistical Abstracts* as distinct categories of offense; arrests for drunken driving are not included in the present table. There are some discrepancies between various editions of the *Abstracts*, the most significant of which is a marriage rate of 5.4 per thousand for 2008 given in the 2011 *Abstract*, rejected here on the grounds that it is much lower than the figures of adjacent years and is corrected in the 2012 *Abstract*. Church membership data are not wholly reliable: they use figures reported by religious denominations, some of which are approximate or out of date, and which often include lapsed members. The 2000 and 2008 figures exclude denominations with fewer than 65,000 and 60,000 members, respectively; in 1980, such denominations accounted for about 0.8 percent of the population. The figure for drug imprisonments in 1930 may be an underestimate; that for 1940 excludes Mississippi and Georgia.
39  Frances Pox Piven and Richard Cloward, *Regulating the Poor: The Functions of Public Welfare* (New York: Pantheon Books, 1971), Introduction.
40  Susan Sheehan, "A Welfare Mother," *New Yorker*, September 29, 1975.
41  Mary E. Richmond, *Friendly Visiting Among the Poor: A Handbook for Charity Workers* (New York: Macmillan, 1899), p. 190.
42  Ibid., p. 191.

43  Ibid., p. 81.

44  Ibid., p. 190.

45  Ibid., p. 193.

46  Charles Loring Brace, *The Best Method of Disposing of Our Pauper and Vagrant Children* (New York: Wynkoop, Hallenbeck & Thomas, 1859), p. 1.

47  Ibid., p. 4.

48  Robert Knickmeyer, "A Marxist View of Social Work," *Social Work*, vol. 17, no. 4 (July 1972), pp. 58–65.

49  Joann Hansen Haggerty, "Pediatric HIV Research," in *Days in the Lives of Social Workers: 58 Professionals Tell "Real-Life" Stories from Social Work Practice*, ed. Linda May Grobman, 4th ed. (Harrisburg, Penn.: White Hat Communications, 2012), p. 95.

50  Michael Crawford, "A Hard Day's Night: Working with Assaultive Men in Prison," in *Days in the Lives of Social Workers*, pp. 254–55.

51  Tyler Cowen, "My Conversation with Bryan Caplan," *Marginal Revolution*, May 9, 2018.

52  Brace, *The Best Method of Disposing of Our Pauper and Vagrant Children*, p. 5.

53  Ibid., p. 11.

54  James Pinkerton, "Mediating Structures, 1977–1995," in Peter Berger and Richard John Neuhaus, *To Empower People: From State to Civil Society*, 20th anniversary edition, ed. Michael Novak (Washington, D.C.: AEI Press, 1996), pp. 55–56.

55  William Galston, "The View from the White House: Individual and Community Empowerment," in *To Empower People*, p. 63.

56  Pinkerton, "Mediating Structures," p. 57.

57  David Kuo, *Tempting Faith: An Inside Story of Political Seduction* (New York: Free Press, 2006), p. xii.

58  Sarah L. Pettijohn and Elizabeth Boris et al., "Nonprofit-Government Contracts and Grants: Findings from the 2013 National Survey," Urban Institute, December 2013.

59  National Institute on Drug Abuse, Overdose Death Rates, January 2019, https://www.drugabuse.gov/related-topics/trends-statistics/overdose-death-rates

60  Daniel Schneider, interview with the author, April 30, 2018.

61  Administration for Children and Families: About: Offices, https://www.acf.hhs.gov/about/offices

62  Richard Gelles, "Creating an Effective Child Welfare System," in *Urban Policy Frontiers* (Manhattan Institute for Policy Research, 2017), p. 59.

63  Richard Gelles, *Out of Harm's Way: Creating an Effective Child Welfare System* (New York: Oxford University Press, 2017).

64  Gelles, "Creating an Effective Child Welfare System," p. 59.

65  Edward D. Berkowitz, *Mr. Social Security: The Life of Wilbur J. Cohen* (Lawrence, Kans.: University Press of Kansas, 1995), p. 282.

66  Joel Schwartz, *Fighting Poverty with Virtue: Moral Reform and America's Urban Poor, 1825–2000* (Bloomington: Indiana University Press, 2000), p. xix.

## CHAPTER 6—GEOFFREY CANADA'S REVIVAL
## OF "MIDDLE-CLASS VALUES"

1 Paul Tough, *Whatever It Takes: Geoffrey Canada's Quest to Change Harlem and America* (Boston: Houghton Mifflin, 2008), pp. 100–1.
2 Geoffrey Canada, *Fist Stick Knife Gun: A Personal History of Violence in America* (Boston: Beacon Press, 1995), pp. 41–42.
3 Ibid., pp. 33–34.
4 Ibid., p. 35.
5 Geoffrey Canada, interview with the author, June 18, 2018. Additional quotations of Canada without citation are from the same interview.
6 Canada, *Fist Stick Knife Gun*, p. 149
7 Tough, *Whatever It Takes*, p. 161.
8 Ibid., p. 101.
9 Ibid., p. 125.
10 Ibid., p. 125.
11 Harlem Children's Zone: Our Results, https://hcz.org/results/
12 Harlem Children's Zone: The Practitioners Institute, https://hcz.org/spreading-the-model/
13 U.S. Department of Education: Programs: Promise Neighborhoods, https://www2.ed.gov/programs/promiseneighborhoods/index.html
14 U.S. Department of Education, "2012 Promise Neighborhoods Competition Opens, $60 Million Available to Continue Reform and Award New Planning and Implementation Grants," Press Release, April 20, 2012.
15 Arne Duncan, "Promise Neighborhoods and the Importance of Community," Remarks of U.S. Secretary of Education Arne Duncan at Neval Thomas Elementary School, Washington, D.C., December 21, 2012, U.S. Department of Education.
16 Lara Hulsey et al., "Promise Neighborhoods Case Studies," Issue Brief, Mathematica Policy Research, December 14, 2015.
17 Lara Hulsey et al., "Promise Neighborhoods Case Studies," Final Report, Mathematica Policy Research, July 2, 2015, p. 32.
18 Ibid., p. 34.
19 Nathan Glazer, *The Limits of Social Policy* (Cambridge, Mass.: Harvard University Press, 1988).
20 Howard Husock, "A Connecticut Yankee in Appalachia," *City Journal*, Spring 2014.

## CONCLUSION—REFLECTIONS ON SOCIAL NORMS

1 Nick Kramer, "Boy Scouts of America Scramble for Membership amid Declining Numbers," TCN News, August 20, 2017.
2 Casey Mulligan, "Redistribution's Second Wave," *Wall Street Journal*, October 2, 2018.
3 Robert Bremner, *From the Depths: The Discovery of Poverty in the United States* (Washington Square: New York University Press, 1956), p. 125, citing Robert Hunter, *Poverty* (1904).

4 Michael B. Katz, *In the Shadow of the Poorhouse: A Social History of Welfare in America* (New York: Basic Books, 1986), p. 71.

5 Deirdre N. McCloskey, *The Bourgeois Virtues* (Chicago: University of Chicago Press, 2006), p. xiv.

6 Joel Schwartz, *Fighting Poverty with Virtue: Moral Reform and America's Urban Poor, 1825–2000* (Bloomington: Indiana University Press, 2000), p. xviii.

7 Daniel Bell, "Foreword: 1978," *The Cultural Contradictions of Capitalism* (1976; New York: Basic Books, 1978), p. xvi.

8 Ibid., p. xx.

9 Ibid., p. xxi.

10 Myron Magnet, *The Dream and the Nightmare: The Sixties' Legacy to the Underclass* (1993; San Francisco: Encounter Books, 2000), p. 1.

11 Kay Hymowitz, *Marriage and Caste in America* (Chicago: Ivan R. Dee, 2006).

12 Jane Addams, "The Objective Value of a Social Settlement," Lecture at the School of Applied Ethics, Plymouth, Mass., 1892, in *Philanthropy and Social Progress* (New York: Thomas Y. Crowell & Co., 1893), pp. 27–40.

# INDEX